GLOBALVIEWPOINTS

Revisiting
Nuclear Power

Other Books of Related Interest

At Issue Series

Nuclear and Toxic Waste

The US Energy Grid

Current Controversies Series

Nuclear Energy

Oil

Introducing Issues with Opposing Viewpoints Series

Energy Alternatives

Nuclear Power

Oil

Issues That Concern You Series

Alternate Energy

Nuclear Power

Opposing Viewpoints Series

Energy Alternatives

Global Resources

Nuclear Power

Revisiting
Nuclear Power

Anne Cunningham, Book Editor

GREENHAVEN
PUBLISHING

Published in 2018 by Greenhaven Publishing, LLC
353 3rd Avenue, Suite 255, New York, NY 10010

Copyright © 2018 by Greenhaven Publishing, LLC

First Edition

Articles in Greenhaven Publishing anthologies are often edited for length to meet page
requirements. In addition, original titles of these works are changed to clearly present
the main thesis and to explicitly indicate the author's opinion. Every effort is made to
ensure that Greenhaven Publishing accurately reflects the original intent of the authors.
Every effort has been made to trace the owners of the copyrighted material.

Cover image: Miguel Villagran/Getty Images
Map: frees/Shutterstock.com

Library of Congress Cataloging-in-Publication Data

Names: Cunningham, Anne C., editor.
Title: Revisiting nuclear power / edited by Anne C. Cunningham.
Description: New York : Greenhaven Publishing, 2018. | Series: Global viewpoints | Includes
bibliographical references and index. | Audience: Grades 9-12.
Identifiers: LCCN ISBN 9781534501294 (library bound) | ISBN 9781534501270 (pbk.)
Subjects: LCSH: Nuclear energy--Juvenile literature. | Nuclear engineering--Juvenile
literature.
Classification: LCC TK9008.N83 2018 | DDC 333.792'4--dc23

Manufactured in the United States of America

Website: http://greenhavenpublishing.com

Contents

Nuclear power should be part of the global energy future. Though nuclear power is potentially clean, reliable, and inexpensive, new plants require high investment, while safety, waste disposal, and weapons proliferation present additional challenges.

Chapter 2: Exploring the Politics of Nuclear Energy

The United States and former Soviet Union created the Nuclear Non-Proliferation Treaty in 1965 to prevent the spread of nuclear weapons. Non-nuclear nations felt this created a two-tiered system enabling the five nuclear-armed nations to maintain their supremacy.

Chapter 3: Nuclear Safety and Security: Critical Issues

Opponents of nuclear energy may overstate the damage caused by Fukushima to promote renewable energy, according to the author. Death rates would have been higher had coal been used to provide Japan with the energy equivalent to nuclear power.

Chapter 4: Is Nuclear Power a Viable Option for the Future?

The probability of a nuclear disaster is quite low, particularly when compared to more likely occurrences such as an automobile accident. However, the consequences inherent in such a catastrophic event are perceived to be extremely high.

The nuclear power industry is once again rebranding itself as a solution to the world's energy and climate problems. However, once the entire fuel cycle and public health is taken into account, nuclear power's promise appears more dubious.

Nuclear power does not live up to its promise. Though the industry touts it as a low-cost, low-risk, and clean fuel, according to Greenpeace the reality is almost the exact opposite.

Foreword

G lobal interdependence has become an undeniable reality. Mass media and technology have increased worldwide access to information and created a society of global citizens. Understanding and navigating this global community is a challenge, requiring a high degree of information literacy and a new level of learning sophistication.

Building on the success of its flagship series, Opposing Viewpoints, Greenhaven Publishing has created the Global Viewpoints series to examine a broad range of current, often controversial topics of worldwide importance from a variety of international perspectives. Providing students and other readers with the information they need to explore global connections and think critically about worldwide implications, each Global Viewpoints volume offers a panoramic view of a topic of widespread significance.

Drugs, famine, immigration—a broad, international treatment is essential to do justice to social, environmental, health, and political issues such as these. Junior high, high school, and early college students, as well as general readers, can all use Global Viewpoints anthologies to discern the complexities relating to each issue. Readers will be able to examine unique national perspectives while, at the same time, appreciating the interconnectedness that global priorities bring to all nations and cultures.

Material in each volume is selected from a diverse range of sources, including journals, magazines, newspapers, nonfiction books, speeches, government documents, pamphlets, organization newsletters, and position papers. Global Viewpoints is truly global, with material drawn primarily from international sources available in English and secondarily from US sources with extensive international coverage.

Features of each volume in the Global Viewpoints series include:

- An **annotated table of contents** that provides a brief summary of each essay in the volume, including the name of the country or area covered in the essay.

- An **introduction** specific to the volume topic.

- A world map to help readers locate the countries or areas covered in the essays.

- For each viewpoint, an **introduction** that contains notes about the author and source of the viewpoint explains why material from the specific country is being presented, summarizes the main points of the viewpoint, and offers three **guided reading questions** to aid in understanding and comprehension.

- **For further discussion** questions that promote critical thinking by asking the reader to compare and contrast aspects of the viewpoints or draw conclusions about perspectives and arguments.

- A worldwide list of **organizations to contact** for readers seeking additional information.

- A **periodical bibliography** and a **bibliography of books** on the volume topic to aid in further research.

- A comprehensive **subject index** to offer access to people, places, events, and subjects cited in the text.

Global Viewpoints is designed for a broad spectrum of readers who want to learn more about current events, history, political science, government, international relations, economics, environmental science, world cultures, and sociology— students doing research for class assignments or debates, teachers and faculty seeking to supplement course materials, and others wanting to understand current issues better. By presenting how people in various countries perceive the root causes, current consequences, and proposed solutions to worldwide challenges, Global Viewpoints volumes offer readers opportunities to enhance their global awareness and their knowledge of cultures worldwide.

Introduction

> *"Many people who have long been
> skeptical about the safety, economic
> feasibility and ultimate morality of
> nuclear power are now somewhat
> willing to consider the argument
> that, at least in the medium term, we
> can't do without it."*
> —Andrew O'Hehir, Salon,
> June 22, 2013.

Nuclear energy stands at a crossroads. Presently, about 20 percent of America's electricity comes from nuclear power. In the popular imagination however, the ominous wide chimney of a nuclear cooling tower is far more closely associated with fears of a devastating meltdown and radioactive waste than with clean, reliable, "green" power. Nuclear power can reduce our dependence on fossil fuels, but a number of dangers and concerns, including aging decrepit plants, high replacement costs, and weapon proliferation risks, impede full public support for a nuclear road forward.

Since its peak in 2006, nuclear power has been in slow decline. The industry has repeatedly come under fire for mismanagement, massive budgets, and long construction times. And of course, there have been disasters of epic proportion, as well as hair-raising near misses. Chernobyl was the worst nuclear accident in history, killing four thousand while exposing more than half a million people to harmful radiation. In 1979, a narrowly averted meltdown at the Three Mile Island nuclear plant in Pennsylvania began turning public opinion against nuclear energy. The plant's location in the densely populated mid-Atlantic region would have made an actual meltdown catastrophic. Luckily, no fatalities occurred, but cleanup costs approaching a billion dollars dampened much enthusiasm for undertaking new nuclear power projects.

Today, many leading environmental advocacy groups such as The Nature Conservancy are reconsidering nuclear power despite the risks. This is because once operational, nuclear plants do provide steady, inexpensive, and reliable electricity with very little carbon emission. Given the scientific consensus that human-caused carbon emission is the primary driver of climate change, nuclear power is once again an attractive option to meet the energy needs of growing populations. We know that burning fossil fuels such as oil, coal, and, to a lesser extent, natural gas for electricity releases carbon dioxide into the atmosphere. Atmospheric concentration of CO_2 is now in excess of four hundred parts per million, a threshold climate scientists have long warned against exceeding. As Naomi Klein discussed at length in her recent book *This Changes Everything*, we only have a few years before this warming trend triggers irreversible feedback loops that could displace millions, and potentially destabilize the globe politically.

Proponents of renewable energy counter that more nuclear energy discourages investment in superior, more sustainable technology. Since many nuclear plants worldwide are on the verge of obsolescence, nuclear power cannot transition us away from fossil fuels without expensive and time-consuming investment in new facilities. By contrast, a utility scale wind farm can be built in two to three years, and at a much cheaper price.

Nuclear power critics also cite the link between civil nuclear technology and weapons proliferation. Very little naturally occurring uranium is viable as nuclear fuel without being enriched. The process by which uranium U-238 is enriched to become reactor fuel also provides material that can be used for nuclear weapons. Reactors also produce plutonium as a by-product of fission. This extremely toxic element can be used in a nuclear weapon as well.

Since the boundary between peaceful nuclear energy and nuclear weapon programs is porous, the international community promotes nuclear energy worldwide at its own peril. Lacking the authority to strictly enforce nonproliferation treaties, the International Atomic Energy Agency and United Nations have little recourse against nations that violate these treaties. North Korea has already withdrawn from both nonproliferation and test ban treaties, and efforts to dissuade Iran from developing a nuclear weapon are fraught with distrust and anxiety. Non-nuclear nations point to the hypocrisy of a two-tiered system allowing some countries to stockpile nuclear weapons without disarmament efforts, while forbidding others to develop the same capabilities. Worse still, the possibility of a rogue actor acquiring a "dirty bomb" remains a serious threat.

The articles comprising this reader all touch on this central question of nuclear energy: can we balance the tremendous output of nuclear power with its considerable risks and disadvantages? While the alternative of doubling-down on fossil fuel is clearly far worse for the planet, many articles that follow view nuclear power as a less than ideal solution to our energy needs. Renewable sources such as solar and wind are arguably cleaner and safer, but as of yet these technologies are unproved on the scale for which they are needed. For example, in recent years Germany has shuttered nuclear plants without generating equivalent power from renewable sources. The country has seen increases in pollution from burning coal and higher energy costs as a result.

Since all sovereign nations have an interest in pursuing energy security and national defense, the critical issues surrounding nuclear energy and weapons are likely to persist. Nuclear power requires prudence and accurate information to realize its potential as an asset, not a liability. The viewpoints included in this volume all contribute to this important goal.

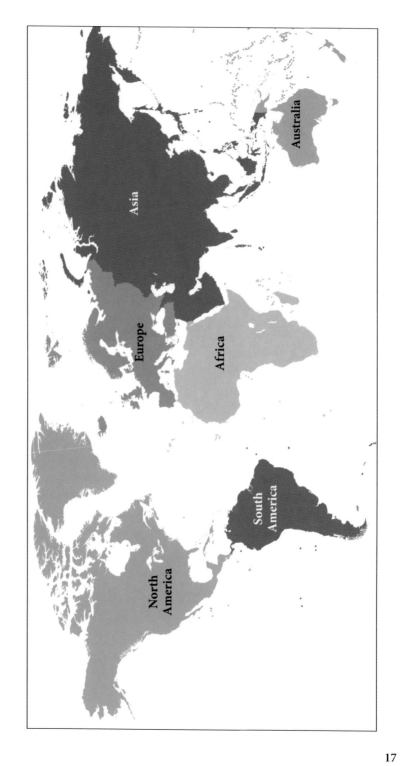

Chapter 1

Nuclear Power Around the World

In Japan, Trust Has Been Lost

Tatsujiro Suzuki

In the following viewpoint, Tatsujiro Suzuki examines Japan's crisis of faith in nuclear power. After a devastating accident at the Fukushima Nuclear Power Plant following an earthquake and tsunami in 2011, the Japanese people questioned the burdens and uncertainty that come with using nuclear power. But, as Suzuki argues, that national sentiment could clash with the current administration's plans for nuclear power to remain a viable energy option. Suzuki is a director and professor at the Research Center for Nuclear Weapons Abolition at Nagasaki University, Japan, and former vice chairman of the Japan Atomic Energy Commission of the Cabinet office.

As you read, consider the following questions:

1. Why was the plan to phase out nuclear power in Japan changed?
2. What does the author consider to be the biggest challenge for Japan and nuclear energy?
3. Where is Japan's supply of separated plutonium located?

Six years have passed since the Fukushima nuclear disaster on March 11, 2011, but Japan is still dealing with its impacts. Decommissioning the damaged Fukushima Daiichi nuclear plant poses unprecedented technical challenges. More than

"Six Years After Fukushima, Much of Japan Has Lost Faith in Nuclear Power," by Tatsujiro Suzuki, The Conversation, March 9, 2017. https://theconversation.com/six-years-after-fukushima-much-of-japan-has-lost-faith-in-nuclear-power-73042. Licensed under CC BY-ND 4.0 International.

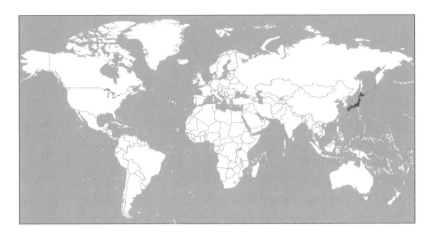

100,000 people were evacuated but only about 13 percent have returned home, although the government has announced that it is safe to return to some evacuation zones.

In late 2016 the government estimated total costs from the nuclear accident at about 22 trillion yen, or about US$188 billion —approximately twice as high as its previous estimate. The government is developing a plan under which consumers and citizens will bear some of those costs through higher electric rates, taxes or both.

The Japanese public has lost faith in nuclear safety regulation, and a majority favors phasing out nuclear power. However, Japan's current energy policy assumes nuclear power will play a role. To move forward, Japan needs to find a new way of making decisions about its energy future.

Uncertainty over nuclear power

When the earthquake and tsunami struck in 2011, Japan had 54 operating nuclear reactors which produced about one-third of its electricity supply. After the meltdowns at Fukushima, Japanese utilities shut down their 50 intact reactors one by one. In 2012 then-Prime Minister Yoshihiko Noda's government announced that it would try to phase out all nuclear power by 2040, after existing plants reached the end of their 40-year licensed operating lives.

Now, however, Prime Minister Shinzo Abe, who took office at the end of 2012, says that Japan "cannot do without" nuclear power. Three reactors have started back up under new standards issued by Japan's Nuclear Regulation Authority, which was created in 2012 to regulate nuclear safety. One was shut down again due to legal challenges by citizens groups. Another 21 restart applications are under review.

In April 2014 the government released its first post-Fukushima strategic energy plan, which called for keeping some nuclear plants as baseload power sources—stations that run consistently around the clock. The plan did not rule out building new nuclear plants. The Ministry of Economy, Trade and Industry (METI), which is responsible for national energy policy, published a long-term plan in 2015 which suggested that nuclear power should produce 20 to 22 percent of Japan's electricity by 2030.

Meanwhile, thanks mainly to strong energy conservation efforts and increased energy efficiency, total electricity demand has been falling since 2011. There has been no power shortage even without nuclear power plants. The price of electricity rose by more than 20 percent in 2012 and 2013, but then stabilized and even declined slightly as consumers reduced fossil fuel use.

Japan's Basic Energy Law requires the government to release a strategic energy plan every three years, so debate over the new plan is expected to start sometime this year.

Public mistrust

The most serious challenge that policymakers and the nuclear industry face in Japan is a loss of public trust, which remains low six years after the meltdowns. In a 2015 poll by the pro-nuclear Japan Atomic Energy Relations Organization, 47.9 percent of respondents said that nuclear energy should be abolished gradually and 14.8 percent said that it should be abolished immediately. Only 10.1 percent said that the use of nuclear energy should be maintained, and a mere 1.7 percent said that it should be increased.

Another survey by the newspaper *Asahi Shimbun* in 2016 was even more negative. Fifty-seven percent of the public opposed restarting existing nuclear power plants even if they satisfied new regulatory standards, and 73 percent supported a phaseout of nuclear power, with 14 percent advocating an immediate shutdown of all nuclear plants.

Who should pay to clean up Fukushima?

METI's 22 trillion yen estimate for total damages from the Fukushima meltdowns is equivalent to about one-fifth of Japan's annual general accounting budget. About 40 percent of this sum will cover decommissioning the crippled nuclear reactors. Compensation expenses account for another 40 percent, and the remainder will pay for decontaminating affected areas for residents.

Under a special financing scheme enacted after the Fukushima disaster, Tepco, the utility responsible for the accident, is expected to pay cleanup costs, aided by favorable government-backed financing. However, with cost estimates rising, the government has proposed to have Tepco bear roughly 70 percent of the cost, with other electricity companies contributing about 20 percent and the government—that is, taxpayers—paying about 10 percent.

This decision has generated criticism both from experts and consumers. In a December 2016 poll by the business newspaper Nihon Keizai Shimbun, one-third of respondents (the largest group) said that Tepco should bear all costs and no additional charges should be added to electricity rates. Without greater transparency and accountability, the government will have trouble convincing the public to share in cleanup costs.

Other nuclear burdens: spent fuel and separated plutonium

Japanese nuclear operators and governments also must find safe and secure ways to manage growing stockpiles of irradiated nuclear fuel and weapon-usable separated plutonium.

At the end of 2016 Japan had 14,000 tons of spent nuclear fuel stored at nuclear power plants, filling about 70 percent of its onsite storage capacity. Government policy calls for reprocessing spent fuel to recover its plutonium and uranium content. But the fuel storage pool at Rokkasho, Japan's only commercial reprocessing plant, is nearly full, and a planned interim storage facility at Mutsu has not started up yet.

The best option would be to move spent fuel to dry cask storage, which withstood the earthquake and tsunami at the Fukushima Daiichi nuclear plant. Dry cask storage is widely used in many countries, but Japan currently has it at only a few nuclear sites. In my view, increasing this capacity and finding a candidate site for final disposal of spent fuel are urgent priorities.

Japan also has nearly 48 tons of separated plutonium, of which 10.8 tons are stored in Japan and 37.1 tons are in France and the United Kingdom. Just one ton of separated plutonium is enough material to make more than 120 crude nuclear weapons.

Many countries have expressed concerns about Japan's plans to store plutonium and use it in nuclear fuel. Some, such as China, worry that Japan could use the material to quickly produce nuclear weapons.

Now, when Japan has only two reactors operating and its future nuclear capacity is uncertain, there is less rationale than ever to continue separating plutonium. Maintaining this policy could increase security concerns and regional tensions, and might spur a "plutonium race" in the region.

As a close observer of Japanese nuclear policy decisions from both inside and outside of the government, I know that change in this sector does not happen quickly. But in my view, the Abe government should consider fundamental shifts in nuclear energy policy to recover public trust. Staying on the current path may undermine Japan's economic and political security. The top priority should be to initiate a national debate and a comprehensive assessment of Japan's nuclear policy.

In Iraq, Nuclear Weapons Have a Dangerous History

Nuclear Threat Initiative

In the following viewpoint, the authors chronicle the history of Iraq's nuclear program from the 1950s through the present. Saddam Hussein sought nuclear weapons until the first gulf war. In 2003, contrary to claims made by the US intelligence community, the International Atomic Energy Agency (IAEA) concluded that little to no evidence existed supporting the assertion that Iraq was pursuing weapons of mass destruction. Saddam Hussein likely exaggerated Iraq's nuclear progress to deter enemies. In the post-Hussein era, Iraq has cooperated with nuclear inspectors, but instability stemming from the rise of ISIS raises new concerns that enriched nuclear materials could slip into the wrong hands and become weapons. The Nuclear Threat Initiative works to prevent catastrophic attacks with weapons of mass destruction and disruption—nuclear, biological, radiological, chemical, and cyber.

As you read, consider the following questions:

1. Has Iraq generally honored its commitments regarding nuclear weapons inspections?
2. What was the extent of Iraq's nuclear program from 1991 to 1998?
3. Are there any unique security concerns with Iraq's nuclear program since the US-led invasion of 2003?

"Nuclear in Iran," Nuclear Threat Initiative, March 2016. Reprinted by permission from James Martin Center for Nonproliferation Studies through the Nuclear Threat Initiative.

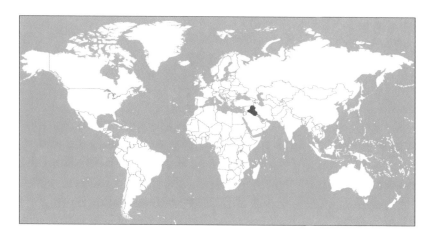

U nder the leadership of Saddam Hussein, Iraq actively pursued nuclear weapons from the early 1970s through 1991. Following the 1991 Gulf War, Iraq's program was subject to unprecedented international oversight under United Nations Security Council (UNSC) Resolution 687, and by 1994 inspectors from the International Atomic Energy Agency (IAEA) who believed they had verified the complete dismantlement of Iraq's nuclear weapons program. [1] In October 1998, Iraq rejected further cooperation with the IAEA, prompting concerns that Iraq might not have abandoned its nuclear weapons ambitions. A second brief inspection process began in November 2002, but it was ultimately cut short by the U.S.-led invasion of Iraq in March 2003. While the Second Gulf War was launched in large part due to concerns that Iraq might have reconstituted its WMD programs, the Iraq Survey Group (ISG) found no evidence that Saddam had reactivated Iraq's nuclear weapons program during the inspection hiatus. [2] The post-Saddam Iraqi government has taken a cooperative stance vis-a-vis the nuclear nonproliferation regime, including by signing the Comprehensive Nuclear Test Ban Treaty (CTBT) and the IAEA Additional Protocol in 2008. However, the recent unrest within Iraq, underlined by the growth of the Islamic State (IS), has given rise to increased concerns over the security of Iraq's remaining nuclear facilities.

History

Early Interest, Israeli Preemption, and
Covert Activities: 1956 to 1990

Iraq's nuclear activities began in 1956, shortly after the commencement of the U.S. Atoms for Peace program, with the establishment of the Iraqi Atomic Energy Commission and its acquisition of a 2MW research reactor, the IRT-5000, from the Soviet Union in 1962. [3] These early activities were likely driven by peaceful intentions, but almost immediately after signing the Treaty on the Non-Proliferation of Nuclear Weapons (NPT) as a non-nuclear weapon state in 1968 and ratifying the treaty a year later, Iraq launched a nuclear weapons program in the early 1970s in violation of its commitments.

During its initial efforts, Iraq pursued the plutonium pathway to the bomb, acquiring two research reactors from France in 1976 (the larger 40MWt Osiraq reactor, or Tammuz I, and the smaller 800KWt Isis reactor, or Tammuz II), as well as a fuel manufacturing facility and a pilot plutonium separation and handling laboratory from the Italian firm SNIA-Techint in 1979. [4] All of these facilities were located at the Tuwaitha Nuclear Research Center near Baghdad, and with the exception of the Italian-supplied "hot cell" plutonium handling facility, were placed under IAEA safeguards. [5] While Iraq's investments were ostensibly directed towards peaceful nuclear activities, Saddam, then Vice President, stated in September 1975 that procurement of a French-built reactor represented, "the first Arab attempt at nuclear arming." [6]

Greatly concerned by Iraq's procurement efforts, Israel bombed the Osiraq facility in June 1981, destroying the reactor core before it was set to come online. According to statements from scientists involved in the program, the attack precipitated a shift in Iraq's strategy, from one based on openly acquiring a latent capability to produce and recover plutonium for weapons to one based on covertly developing a uranium enrichment capability at undeclared facilities. [7] Over the next decade Iraq pursued several enrichment methods, including electromagnetic isotope separation (EMIS), gaseous diffusion, and gas-centrifuges.

The EMIS project received priority attention for much of the 1980s, and in 1987 Iraq contracted a Yugoslav firm to build a facility in Al-Tarmiya north of Baghdad capable of producing 15 kilograms of weapons-grade uranium per year. [8] That same year, Iraq also decided to build a second, replica EMIS facility at Ash Sharqat, northwest of Baghdad. Work on the gaseous diffusion method began at Tuwaitha in 1982, but was subsequently moved to a site near Rashdiya in northern Baghdad. Iraq hoped this effort could produce low enriched uranium (LEU) feedstock for further enrichment in the EMIS program, but due to difficulties in machining precision components, the gaseous diffusion project was abandoned in 1987 or 1988 in favor of gas-centrifuges. [9] Although centrifuges were originally deemed too difficult to develop, Iraq was able to make significant headway in the late 1980s with assistance from centrifuge experts associated with West German firms. [10] Concurrent with its work on uranium enrichment, Iraq also conducted extensive research on nuclear weapon design and assembly, primarily at the Al-Atheer and Al Qa Qaa complexes. [11]

Despite this progress, Saddam, facing the prospect of a U.S.-led response to Iraq's invasion of Kuwait, was forced to alter his plans and initiate a "crash program" to acquire fissile material for nuclear weapons. Codenamed Project 601, Iraqi scientists were directed in August 1990 to recover safeguarded highly enriched uranium (HEU) from French- and Russian-supplied research reactors. [12] According to the IAEA, had the crash program been successful, Iraq would have been able to extract around 25 kg of HEU, which "could have resulted in the availability by the end of 1991 of a quantity of HEU sufficient to manufacture a single low-yield nuclear device." [13] Coalition bombing unknowingly hampered this effort by destroying many of Iraq's facilities and diverting Iraqi attention away from the nuclear program. [14]

International Inspections Reveal the Extent of Iraq's Program: 1991 to 1998

Following the end of the Gulf War in 1991, UNSC Resolution 687 directed the IAEA to find and dismantle Iraq's nuclear weapons program, and ensure Iraqi compliance with the NPT through comprehensive ongoing monitoring and verification. Despite this broad and unprecedented mandate, the IAEA initially received only minimal cooperation from Iraq. In its first declaration to the IAEA, Iraq failed to disclose the existence of EMIS uranium enrichment facilities at Al-Tarmiya and Ash Sharqat, as well as its weaponization research. Nevertheless, inspections revealed much of the program and forced Iraq to admit to its weapons aspirations, including research at Tuwaitha and Al-Atheer. [15]

Between May 1991 and October 1997 the IAEA completed a series of 30 inspection campaigns, oversaw the destruction and disablement of nuclear facilities, and removed all weapons-usable nuclear material from Iraq. [16] Other nuclear materials were accounted for and placed under the IAEA's control, including some 500 tons of natural uranium and approximately 1.8 tons of low enriched uranium dioxide. [17] By 1994, the IAEA's campaign to incapacitate Iraq's nuclear program through "destruction, removal, and rendering harmless" of its nuclear facilities and materials was complete. [18] IAEA inspections were reinforced by information from two prominent members of the Iraqi nuclear program, Hussein Kamel and Khidir Hamza, both of whom defected in the mid-1990s and provided the IAEA and the UN Special Commission (UNSCOM) with a more coherent picture of Iraq's program. [19] Kamel and Hamza's revelations included evidence of Iraq's "crash program," its work on EMIS technology, and its use of declassified data from the U.S. Manhattan Project. [20]

Through late 1998 the IAEA continued to monitor Iraq's nuclear activities despite the regime's reluctance to cooperate fully. Following Saddam's announcement in October 1998 that he would end all cooperation with UN inspectors, UNSCOM Chairman Richard Butler issued a scathing report to the UNSC detailing

Iraq's efforts to obstruct the commission's mandate. [21] The report became the basis for the December 1998 U.S. and British bombing campaign known as Operation Desert Fox. [22] IAEA and UN inspectors withdrew from Iraq that same month, and Saddam did not permit their reentry for another four years.

The Iraq War and its Aftermath: 2003 to 2010
In January 2001, a U.S. Defense Department report assessed that "Iraq would need five or more years and key foreign assistance to rebuild the infrastructure to enrich enough material for a nuclear weapon," adding that the amount of time needed could be "substantially shortened" if Iraq obtained fissile material from a foreign source. [23] Facing the prospect of a U.S. invasion and claims that it had weapons of mass destruction, Iraq permitted IAEA inspectors to resume verification activities within the country. Although Iraq retained its nuclear expertise, including design information, scientists and engineers, and a powerful and effective concealment apparatus, IAEA Director General Mohamed El-Baradei reported to the UNSC on 7 March 2003 that "After three months of intrusive inspections, we have to date found no evidence or plausible indications of the revival of a nuclear weapon program in Iraq." [24]

After the Second Gulf War, which removed Saddam from power in April 2003, the U.S. Central Intelligence Agency's Iraq Survey Group (ISG) was tasked with uncovering evidence of Iraq's alleged illicit WMD programs. In its comprehensive report issued on 30 September 2004, the ISG concluded there was no evidence to suggest that a coordinated effort to restart Iraq's nuclear program had existed since the first Gulf War ended in 1991. [25] Inspectors instead found that Saddam Hussein had planned to recreate his WMD programs after the lifting of international sanctions. The ISG report states that as early as 1991, Saddam told his advisors he wanted to continue to employ Iraq's nuclear scientists, a theme the report claims "persisted throughout the sanctions period." [26] However, since Iraq lacked the ability to continue the program at its full potential, Saddam instead sought to deter adversaries by falsely aggrandizing Iraq's overall WMD capabilities. [27]

As a result of the ISG's findings, the United States Congress arranged for a Senate Committee inquiry into the U.S. intelligence community's prewar assessments on Iraq. In a formal report released in March 2005, the committee accused the intelligence community of using insufficient sources, being too wedded to previous assumptions, and failing to conduct substantial research on the issues. The report states the intelligence community was "almost completely wrong" in its assumptions about Iraq's nuclear program. [28] Most intelligence agencies faced accusations about their failures prior to the invasion, including the National Security, Central Intelligence, Defense Intelligence, and National Geospatial-Intelligence Agencies.

Recent Developments and Current Status

The post-Saddam Iraqi government has taken several noteworthy steps to demonstrate its support for the nonproliferation regime, including ratification of the IAEA Additional Protocol and the CTBT in 2012 and 2013, respectively. Prior actions, including Iraq's provisional implementation of the Additional Protocol, led the UNSC to lift Saddam-era restrictions on its nuclear activities in December 2010. [29]

After years of inspections, sanctions, and conflict, Iraq's nuclear capabilities are now limited to medical and agricultural applications. Citing research interests and a growing demand for electricity, former Iraqi Minister of Science and Technology Raed Fahmi announced in 2009 that Iraq would explore the feasibility of developing a peaceful nuclear program. [30] Given domestic instability and cost considerations, however, the current Iraqi government is not pursuing nuclear power or other nuclear technologies at this time.

Iraq has also worked in cooperation with international partners through the Iraq Nuclear Facility Dismantlement and Disposal Project to eliminate most of Iraq's remaining nuclear infrastructure, much of which poses health and security risks. [31] Indeed, widespread unrest and looting, including from nuclear facilities in the wake of the 2003 Iraq War, created concerns that nuclear and other radioactive materials as well as dual-use technologies could fall into the hands of extremist groups. [32] Such concerns have become more acute with the escalation of activities by the Islamic State (IS), a terrorist group that has seized large swathes of territory in eastern Syria and across northern and western Iraq. In July 2014, IS reportedly seized approximately 40 kilograms of uranium compounds from a scientific university in the northern city of Mosul. [33] However, the IAEA noted that the material was "low grade and would not present a significant safety, security or nuclear nonproliferation risk." [34] Others have supported the IAEA's risk assessment. Unless IS stole other unreported material, they most likely only possess low-enriched or natural uranium. Both forms of uranium pose a low radioactive risk, even if deployed in radiological dispersal devices such as dirty bombs. [35] If IS does control other radioactive materials confiscated within its territory, such as those commonly found in hospitals and clinics, those materials would be most relevant for inflicting mass disruption, and for causing fear and panic. [36] Baghdad concluded an agreement with the United States shortly after the ISIS theft on a "Joint Action Plan to Combat Nuclear and Radioactive Smuggling" in September 2014, demonstrating both sides' concerns that the civil war in neighboring Syria and the domestic turmoil within Iraq will create ongoing security challenges for Iraq's remaining nuclear installations. [37]

Sources

[1] Federation of American Scientists, "IAEA and Iraqi Nuclear Weapons," www.fas.org.
[2] Comprehensive Report of the Special Advisor to the DCI on Iraq's WMD," Central Intelligence Agency, No. 2, p. 7, September 30, 2004, www.cia.gov.
[3] Etel Solingen, *Nuclear Logics: Contrasting Paths is East Asia & The Middle East* (Princeton: Princeton University Press, 2007), p. 143.
[4] Etel Solingen, *Nuclear Logics: Contrasting Paths is East Asia & The Middle East* (Princeton: Princeton University Press, 2007), p. 143.
[5] Roger Richter, "Testimony form a former safeguards inspector," *Bulletin of the Atomic Scientists* Vol. 37 (1981): 29, accessed September 12, 2014, www.isis-online.org.

[6] Jeffrey T. Richelson, *Spying on the Bomb*, (New York: Norton, 2007), p. 321.

[7] Steve Weissman and Herbert Krosney, *The Islamic Bomb; the Nuclear Threat to Israel and the Middle East* (New York, NY: Times Books, 1981), pp. 227-233. Jeffrey T. Richelson, Spying on the Bomb, (New York: Norton, 2007), p. 323.

[8] David Albright, "Iraq's Program to Make Highly Enriched Uranium and Plutonium for Nuclear Weapons Prior to the Gulf War, The Institute for Science and International Security, October 9. 2002 www.iraqwatch.org; Jeffrey T. Richelson, Spying on the Bomb, (New York: Norton, 2007), p. 322.

[9] Jeffrey T. Richelson, *Spying on the Bomb*, (New York: Norton, 2007), p. 324.

[10] David Albright, "Iraq's Program to Make Highly Enriched Uranium and Plutonium for Nuclear Weapons Prior to the Gulf War," The Institute for Science and International Security, October 9, 2002, www.iraqwatch.org.

[11] Jeffrey T. Richelson, *Spying on the Bomb*, (New York: Norton, 2007), p. 349; Federation of American Scientists, "IAEA and Iraqi Nuclear Weapons," www.fas.org.

[12] IAEA, "Report on the Twenty-Eighth IAEA on-site Inspection in Iraq under Security Council Resolution 687 (1991)," S/1995/1003, December 1, 1995, www.iaea.org.

[13] IAEA, "Report on the Twenty-Eighth IAEA on-site Inspection in Iraq under Security Council Resolution 687 (1991)," S/1995/1003, December 1, 1995, www.iaea.org; IAEA, "The Implementation of United Nations Security Council Resolutions Relating to Iraq," (GC(40)/1), August 12, 1996, www.iaea.org.

[14] David Albright, "Iraq's Program to Make Highly Enriched Uranium and Plutonium for Nuclear Weapons Prior to the Gulf War," The Institute for Science and International Security, October 9, 2002, www.iraqwatch.org.

[15] Global Security, "IAEA and Iraqi Nuclear Weapons," www.globalsecurity.org.

[16] Mohamed ElBaradei, *The Age of Deception: Nuclear Diplomacy in Treacherous Times*, (New York: Metropolitan Books, 2011), p. 31.

[17] Garry B. Dillon, "The IAEA Iraq Action Team Record: Activities and Findings," in *Iraq: A New Approach*, Washington, D.C.: Carnegie Endowment for International Peace, August 2002, p. 41, www.carnegieendowment.org.

[18] United Nations Security Council, *Fourth Consolidated report of the Director General of the International Atomic Energy Agency under paragraph 16 of Security Council Resolution 1051 (1996)*, S/1997/779, October 8, 1997, p. 16, www.iaea.org; Garry B. Dillon, "The IAEA Iraq Action Team Record: Activities and Findings," in *Iraq: A New Approach*, Washington, D.C.: Carnegie Endowment for International Peace, August 2002, p. 41, www.carnegieendowment.org.

[19] Jacques Baute, "Timeline Iraq: Challenges & Lessons Learned from Nuclear Inspections," IAEA Bulletin 46/1, June 2004.

[20] IAEA, "Report of the fourth IAEA inspection in Iraq under Security Council resolution 687," S/24593, 31 August - 7 September 1992; Federation of American Scientists, "Iraq's Nuclear Weapons Program: From Aflaq to Tammuz."

[21] Mohamed ElBaradei, *The Age of Deception: Nuclear Diplomacy in Treacherous Times*, (New York: Metropolitan Books, 2011), p. 34; Jeffrey T. Richelson, *Spying on the Bomb*, (New York: Norton, 2007), p. 469.

[22] Mohamed ElBaradei, *The Age of Deception: Nuclear Diplomacy in Treacherous Times*, (New York: Metropolitan Books, 2011), p. 34; Jeffrey T. Richelson, *Spying on the Bomb*, (New York: Norton, 2007), p. 469.

[23] U.S. Department of Defense, "Proliferation: Threat and Response," January 2001, p. 40; Joseph Cirincione with Jon B. Wolfsthal and Miraiam Rajkumar, *Deadly Arsenals: Tracking Weapons of Mass Destruction*, (Washington, DC: Carnegie, 2005), pp. 273-275.

[24] Mohamad ElBaradei, "Statement to the UN Security Council," March 7, 2003, www. iaea.org.

[25] "Comprehensive Report of the Special Advisor to the DCI on Iraq's WMD," Central Intelligence Agency, No. 1, p. 24, September 30, 2004, www.cia.gov.

[26] "Comprehensive Report of the Special Advisor to the DCI on Iraq's WMD," Central Intelligence Agency, No. 2, p. 1, September 30, 2004, www.cia.gov.

[27] "Comprehensive Report of the Special Advisor to the DCI on Iraq's WMD," Central Intelligence Agency, No. 1, p. 28, September 30, 2004, www.cia.gov.

[28] The Commission on the Intelligence Capabilities of the United States Regarding Weapons of Mass Destruction, *Report to the President of the United States*, March 31, 2005, pp. 8-9.

[29] United Nations Security Council, "Resolution 1957 (2010)," December 15, 2010, www.un.org.

[30] Martin Chulov, "Iraq goes nuclear with plans for new reactor programme," The Guardian, October 27, 2009.

[31] Federation of American Scientists, "Iraqi Nuclear Weapons," www.fas.org.

[32] Charles D. Ferguson and William C. Potter, *The Four Faces of Nuclear Terrorism*, (Monterey: Center for Nonproliferation Studies, Monterey Institute of International Studies, 2004), pp. 271-274; Louis Charbonneau, "U.N. fears bombmakers may get Iraq nuke items - diplomats," *Reuters*, October 12, 2004.

[33] Michelle Nichols, "Iraq tells U.N. that 'terrorist groups' seized nuclear materials," Reuters, July 9, 2014.

[34] Alan Cowell, "'Low-Grade Nuclear Material Is Seized by Rebels," *The New York Times*, July 10, 2014.

[35] George Moore, "Is ISIL a Radioactive Threat?" *Federation of American Scientists*, November 7, 2014, www.fas.org.

[36] George Moore, "Is ISIL a Radioactive Threat?" *Federation of American Scientists*, November 7, 2014, www.fas.org.

[37] U.S. Department of State, "U.S. and Iraq Sign a Joint Action Plan to Combat Nuclear and Radioactive Smuggling," Press Release, September 3, 2014, www.state.gov.

In North Korea, Nuclear Weapons Are the Key to Security

Zack Beauchamp

In the following viewpoint, Zack Beauchamp examines the development of nuclear weapons in North Korea. Since North Korea historically relied on the Soviet Union for economic aid and protection, the collapse of the Soviet Union in 1989 left North Korea especially vulnerable. In 1993, North Korea withdrew from the Nonproliferation Treaty (NPT). At the same time, a new ideology called Songun elevated the military to supremacy, even as many citizens starved. To this day, North Korea has staked its future on nuclear weapons in the face of sanctions, despite less than encouraging success rates in their nuclear tests. Beauchamp is world correspondent at Vox.

As you read, consider the following questions:

1. Why is North Korea so invested in a nuclear weapons program?
2. Contrast the strategies of Presidents Bill Clinton and George W. Bush in dealing with North Korea's nuclear program?
3. Does North Korea possess the capability to strike the United States with nuclear weapons?

Very late on Tuesday, North Korea claimed that it had tested a hydrogen bomb, an especially powerful type of nuclear

"A Brief History Of North Korea's Nuclear Program And the Failed US Campaign To Stop It," by Zack Beauchamp, Vox Media Inc., January 7, 2016. Reprinted by permission.

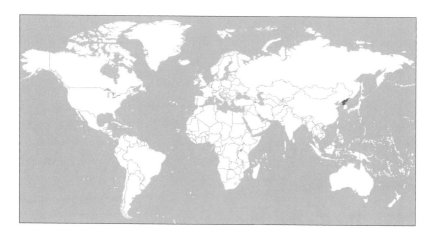

weapon. Experts are skeptical that the North Koreans actually detonated a full hydrogen bomb, but the evidence does suggest that some kind of smaller nuclear weapon went off.

To understand why North Korea would do this, why it even has a nuclear program, and what this program means for it and the world, you need to understand the history of North Korea's program: where it came from and how it's changed over the years. So here's a brief guide to that program, written to help you put Tuesday's test in context.

1991: The collapse of the Soviet Union

From the division of the Korean Peninsula and the creation of North Korea in 1945 up until 1991, Moscow was its ally and sponsor. The Soviets provided North Korea with huge amounts of economic aid and security assistance, propping up the country. As a superpower patron, the Soviets also provided North Korea with diplomatic and military support.

So when the Soviet Union began collapsing in 1989, and ultimately dissolved in 1991, North Korea was left in a precarious position. China filled in the void somewhat, but the North knew that China had no real affection for it and so wouldn't provide the same level of protection as the Soviet Union did.

This is why Johns Hopkins's Joel Wit and Sun Young Ahn date the origins of North Korea's modern nuclear program to 1989 (the regime had done nuclear research as early as the 1950s).

"With the collapse of the Soviet Union, North Korea lost its main protector. Its turn to developing nuclear weapons made a lot of sense," Keir Lieber, a professor at Georgetown who has studied the thinking behind North Korea's nuclear program, told me. "What does it have that can counter conventional US power? The answer is obvious: nuclear weapons."

1994: The Clinton administration makes a deal with North Korea

The international crisis over North Korea's nuclear program has been around almost as long as North Korea's modern nuclear program. In March 1993, the country announced it would withdraw from the Non-Proliferation Treaty (NPT), which bars non-nuclear states from starting nuclear weapons programs. A month later, the International Atomic Energy Agency (IAEA) said it could no longer verify that North Korea was using its nuclear material for peaceful purposes.

The Clinton administration sat down with North Korea to try to negotiate a deal that would prevent it from acquiring nuclear weapons. In 1994, the US and North Korea announced a deal called the Agreed Framework. North Korea agreed to dismantle its nuclear reactors and accept wide-ranging inspections in exchange for diplomatic and economic concessions from the United States.

From North Korea's point of view, this was a way to take advantage of its nuclear program without actually building nukes. "Pyongyang chose to capitalize on the political and diplomatic utility of nuclear weapons by accepting crippling limits on its plutonium-based fissile material program in return for a better relationship with the United States that would diminish external security threats," Wit and Ahn explain.

But the deal was far from an inevitable success. In order for it to work, North Korea had to continue believing that adhering to the deal was a better way to protect North Korea's security interests than flouting it would be. And this didn't last forever.

1994–1998: North Korea's famine and the Songun policy

In 1994, North Korea's longtime dictator Kim Il Sung died and was succeeded by his son, Kim Jong Il. At the same time, North Korea suffered a famine so severe that much of the population died. (Reliable estimates of the famine's death toll are hard to come by, but estimates range between 600,000 and 2.5 million during the '90s.). The collapse in Soviet aid and trade after 1991, together with a series of droughts and floods in the early '90s, collapsed North Korea's food provision system. What happened next is very important to understanding North Korea, and the nuclear program in particular.

Faced with a question of how to secure the North Korean state in the wake of the Soviet collapse, new leader Kim Jong Il developed something called the Songun, or military-first, doctrine. Songun differed from previous North Korean ideology in that it put the military at the heart of the North Korean state.

Under Songun, "the military is not just an institution designed to perform the function of defending the country from external hostility," South Korean scholar Han S. Park writes. "Instead, it provides all of the other institutions of the government with legitimacy."

On this theory, North Koreans' dire poverty is a necessary condition of the state's strength, not a problem. The military needs everything society has to offer in order to protect North Korea from outsiders; civilians' sacrifices are necessary to preserve the state that protects them.

The practical effect of Songun was that the military got all resources first—including rations during the famine while the rest of North Korea starved.

What does this have to do with the nuclear program? It illustrates just how central militarism became to North Korean strategic doctrine—and because the state thus needed an external threat to justify Songun and the civilian sacrifices it called for. The Kim regime clearly concluded that even in the face of utter economic calamity, fully funding the military was the key to the regime's continued survival. Convincing the people that the military was their savior, not economic or social reform, would allow the North Korean regime to stay in place.

That explains why the North, in the coming years, became so attached to the idea of a nuclear weapon. If the nation's legitimacy depended on the vitality of its military, then acquiring the world's most powerful military weapon became important for more than just foreign policy reasons. It was also a way to show the North Korean people that their military was a powerful protector they could count on for their security.

1998: North Korea tests a long-range missile

In November 2015, North Korea fired a test missile of a new type, called the Taepodong-1—over Japan. This new missile's maximum range was roughly twice that of the North's next-biggest weapon, the Rodong.

This kind of medium-range missile could potentially hold a nuclear payload, if North Korea figured out how to both build and then miniaturize a nuclear bomb. As such, the international community saw this as a profound provocation: Testing a nuclear-capable weapon at a time when negotiations over North Korea's nuclear and ballistic missile programs were still ongoing suggested a clear lack of intent to adhere to the deal's spirit and perhaps letter.

The Taepodong-1 test reveals two important things about the North Korean program. First, North Korea is quite willing to provoke the West when it wants to, even if it jeopardizes international negotiations. This could be either because North Korea is trying to extract concessions or simply because it wants to strengthen its military; scholars disagree. But the point is that it's not obvious how committed North Korea ever was to good-faith negotiations.

"Even in 1994, there's still a question as to whether North Korea was ever committed to abiding by the Agreed Framework," Lieber told me.

Second, North Korea lies about its technological capabilities—a lot. North Korean state media claimed the Taepodong launch put a satellite into orbit; independent data suggested no such satellite reached orbit. It looked like North Korea had tried to send up a satellite, but the object had most likely been blown up when its own fuel tank exploded.

This may seem ridiculous, given that it's easy to verify whether North Korea is lying about stuff like this. But it actually makes a certain amount of sense: North Korea maintains a really tight grip on the media domestically. Exaggerating its military strength helps make the military stronger, thus solidifying the regime's legitimacy in Songun terms.

2001: Bush takes office, US policy shifts

When George W. Bush became president, America's North Korea policy shifted dramatically. While the Clinton administration took an essentially carrot-and-stick approach to North Korea's nuclear program—if you give them some stuff, and threaten other stuff, maybe you can shape their behavior—the Bush team disdained negotiations.

"At its outset, the Bush Administration was generally disinclined to test the incentives-for-denuclearization hypothesis that the Clinton team had explored," Evans J.R. Revere, a Korea expert at Brookings, writes. "Many in the new administration were convinced that North Korea had no intention of giving up its nuclear program at any price. Many were also opposed in principle to providing incentives or 'rewards' to North Korea, a regime they detested, even if this might yield some progress."

As a result, the Agreed Framework—always on tenuous footing given the nature of the North Korean regime—collapsed. "Before the end of 2002, North Korea removed the seals on the 5-megawatt reactor and other facilities at Yongbyon, evicted IAEA monitors, and began the process of restarting its nuclear weapons program," Revere explains.

According to Revere, some Bush officials internally advocated for renewing negotiations, and by 2003 they succeeded. The US and four other interested powers (South Korea, Japan, China, and Russia)—sat down with North Korea to discuss a nuclear agreement. They made some progress: In 2005, North Korea agreed in principle to give up its nuclear weapons program.

But the new agreement, unlike the Agreed Framework, didn't involve temporarily freezing North Korea's nuclear weapons while a final agreement was hashed out. As negotiations dragged on, North Korean research on a bomb continued.

You can read this one of two ways. You could say the Bush administration screwed up a good thing the Clinton team had put in place. Or you could say it showed that North Korea had entered negotiations in bad faith and was always going to pursue a bomb regardless.

Revere thinks it's the latter: "In retrospect, the US inability to attain [an end to the program] owes much more to North Korea's dogged determination to possess nuclear weapons than to any other factor," he concludes.

It probably didn't help, though, that the Bush administration had launched an invasion of Iraq to topple Saddam Hussein for his supposed weapons of mass destruction—and that Bush had named North Korea alongside Iraq as part of the "axis of evil," perhaps contributing to North Korea's desire for a nuclear deterrent.

2006: North Korea tests its first nuclear weapon

This was the year everything went to hell. In July, North Korea tested the Taepodong-2, its first missile that could theoretically reach parts of the United States—if it had worked, anyway. The test failed, but it raised serious concern about North Korea's intentions.

Then on October 9, North Korea tested its first nuclear device near the village of Punggye-ri.

The device was primitive. It boasted a single kiloton of explosive power at most; the bomb dropped on Hiroshima, detonated more than 60 years prior, yielded somewhere between 13 and 18 kilotons.

But it nonetheless changed the game. Any negotiations would have to start from the fact that North Korea already possessed nuclear weapons rather than attempting to prevent that from happening.

After the test, North Korea signaled that it would be open to denuclearization in official statements. The UN Security Council passed a resolution condemning the test, which also imposed new economic sanctions on North Korea.

The big question then became: How much did North Korea value its hard-won nuclear capability? And would it be willing to give it up in exchange for a relaxation?

2009: North Korea's second nuclear test

This question was answered rather decisively in May 2009, when North Korea tested its second nuclear device. This bomb showed modest technological progress, with a yield estimated to be between 2 and 8 kilotons. But the most important element of the test was the signal: North Korea was, clearly, still committed to expanding its nuclear arsenal.

The UN Security Council slapped more sanctions on North Korea, but it was hard to give them much bite. North Korea's economy was already broken, having been walled off from most international trade since the end of the Cold War. Clearly, the Kim regime was willing to suffer international isolation and economic deprivation in the name of preserving its nuclear arsenal.

This, in essence, has been the status quo for North Korea nuclear policy ever since. The North Koreans aren't willing to give up their weapons now that they've built them, and there's just not a whole lot the United States or South Korea can do to punish them for the program. The Obama administration has attempted to revive Clinton-style negotiations but, given the contours of the situation, haven't made it a top priority à la negotiations with Iran.

So the North Korean program keeps on chugging.

"We already don't have diplomatic relations; we've already sanctioned them multiple times," David Kang, a professor at the University of Southern California, told me in an interview last year. "There's not much you can do."

2012: North Korea's missile test fails dramatically

In 2012, North Korea test-launched an Unha-3, a rocket derived from the Taepodong-2 that could serve as a prelude to an even bigger missile. Only the test failed yet again: The missile disintegrated right after launch. The failure was so embarrassing that even the North Korean state media couldn't cover it up; according to the New York Times, "it was the first time the North has publicly acknowledged a long-range missile or satellite failure."

This points to something important: North Korean mastery of nuclear and related missile technology is still thought to be quite rudimentary. While the program poses a very real threat to its neighbors, particularly Japan and South Korea, we don't actually know how may weapons it has or how effective its delivery mechanisms (bombers, submarines) are. What we do know publicly, though, is that North Korea has a long track record of technological failure.

Take, for instance, the persistent claim that North Korea has nuclear missiles that can hit the United States. This comes from the theoretical range of the Taepodong-2 missile, which at its peak could hit Alaska. But the Taepodong-2 has never demonstrated that kind of reach in an actual test, nor has North Korea demonstrated that it can make a nuclear device small enough to fit on a warhead (though it's conceivable).

North Korea "has had tremendous trouble overcoming various technical hurdles that US experts assumed would not pose any serious difficulties at all," Jacques Hymans, another USC professor, said in a 2013 interview with the Federation of American Scientists. "Even its recent tests can be said to have been 'successful' only relative to the ridiculously low bar that Pyongyang had set with its prior disastrous test failures."

2013: North Korea's third nuclear test

In 2013, North Korea tested its third nuclear device (this time with a 6 or 7 kiloton yield). This test raised yet another question: If North Korea already had nuclear weapons, why would it need to keep testing them?

There are a number of possible answers. Maybe it was a provocation designed to wring concessions from the West. It's also easy to read this through the lens of Songun: North Korea needs to keep demonstrating military advances, even fictional advances, to show the people that the military is strong enough to protect them.

But there's a third, simpler explanation, one advanced by Dartmouth professors Jennifer Lind and Daryl Press, along with Lieber, in Foreign Affairs. Writing after this third test, they argued that the right answer was probably the simplest one: These are, in fact, tests designed to improve the quality of North Korea's nuclear arsenal.

This, the scholars note, has historical precedent. "Between 1945 and 1992, the United States conducted 1,054 nuclear tests and fired an untold number of missiles. If the goal had merely been to show the Soviets that the United States meant business, testing nearly twice a month throughout the entire Cold War would have been overkill," they write.

Instead, they claim, North Korea believes its security depends on nuclear weapons, and thus needs to make sure they work. "North Korea's mission requires small, lightweight warheads, and missiles that work," Lind et al. write. "The only way to know that they work is to test them."

2016: North Korea tests a fourth bomb—and claims it's hydrogen

In December 2015, North Korea claimed something that seemed incredible: It had built a hydrogen bomb, which is a more advanced form of nuclear weapon. Then on January 6, after a seismic anomaly occurred within North Korean territory, the country claimed to have actually tested one.

"The DPRK's access to H-bomb of justice ... is the legitimate right of a sovereign state for self-defense and a very just step no one can slander," an official statement from the state-run Korean Central News Agency blared.

Hydrogen bombs work by harnessing energy created by fusing hydrogen atoms together, unlike atomic bombs, which work by tearing apart atoms through atomic fission. This makes hydrogen bombs much more powerful.

"Nuclear weapons employing fusion can have a yield measured in megatons. (A kiloton is 1,000 tons; a megaton is 1,000 kilotons)," Bruce Bennett, a defense analyst at the RAND Corporation, explains in a piece for CNN published when North Korea first claimed to have developed a fusion bomb.

If North Korea had developed a hydrogen bomb, this would be a big step up technologically. But experts were very, very skeptical: The size of the seismic disturbance created by the bomb was similar to past tests, and thus too small to be made by a bomb that was orders of magnitude more powerful.

However, it is possible North Korea is using a sort of in-between weapon called a "boosted" nuclear device. This involves a very small amount of fusion to boost the explosive capability of a fission bomb. According to Bennett, these weapons generally have a yield around 50 kilotons.

"Maybe boosted. Definitely not a successful staged device," Jeffrey Lewis, the director of the East Asia Nonproliferation Program at the Middlebury Institute of International Studies, tweeted.

Regardless, the test shows that North Korea's nuclear knowhow is still expanding (however slowly). "Whatever the type of design of weapon tested by North Korea or its exact yield, this fourth nuclear test has undoubtedly advanced North Korea's technical understanding of their nuclear designs," the Arms Control Association's Daryl Kimball and Kelsey Davenport write.

And there doesn't seem to be a thing anyone can do about it.

In Iran, Nuclear Ambitions Are Cause for International Concern

David Albright and Andrea Stricker

In the the following viewpoint, David Albright and Andrea Stricker trace Iran's nuclear history. This began peacefully, with the United States selling Iran a small research reactor in the 1950s. By 1974, the Shah established the Atomic Energy Organization of Iran (AEOI) for civilian use, but wished to retain control over the nuclear fuel cycle for possible weapons. After the Iranian revolution, Iran briefly paused its nuclear program, which resumed during the Iran-Iraq war. Despite many subsequent inspections and pressure from the EU 3 (Britain, France, and Germany), Iran has retained nuclear facilities that could lead to weapons development. The 2015 nuclear deal with the United States stalled these efforts, but perhaps only temporarily. Albright, a physicist and former UN weapons inspector, is the president and founder of the Institute for Science and International Security (ISIS) in Washington, DC. Stricker is a senior policy analyst at the Institute for Science and International Security (ISIS).

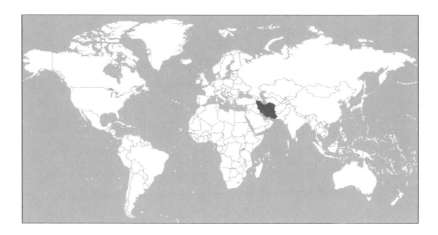

As you read, consider the following questions:

1. How did Iran's nuclear program progress to the point that the international community suspected possible weapons?
2. What was revealed in 2002 that suggested Iran's nuclear weapons program was intact?
3. How would you characterize the framework of the United States–Iran nuclear deal?

- Since the 1970s, even before the revolution, Iran has sought access to the technology that would give it the option to build a nuclear bomb, should it believe its security situation requires it.

- Iran intensified its drive toward nuclear weapons in the 1980s during the Iran-Iraq War, following reports of an Iraqi clandestine nuclear program.

- Iranian leaders advanced Iran's nuclear weapons program in the 1990s and early 2000s along with its civil nuclear program, using the latter as a symbol of national pride. They denied that Iran's nuclear program ever had a military purpose despite substantial evidence possessed by the International Atomic Energy Agency and national intelligence agencies that it conducted nuclear weapons related work up until 2003 and perhaps continued certain activities afterwards.

- As a signatory to the Nuclear Non-Proliferation Treaty, Iran claims its nuclear program has always been purely for peaceful energy and medical purposes.

- In November 2013, Iran signed an interim agreement limiting its nuclear programs—the Joint Plan of Action—with six world powers, the P5+1 (Britain, China, France, Germany, Russia and the United States).

- On July 14, 2015, Iran and the P5+1 concluded a comprehensive deal with key provisions to limit Iran's nuclear programs for 10 to 15 years and improve international transparency over its activities, in exchange for a removal of U.N., regional, and national sanctions. The agreement, known as the Joint Comprehensive Plan of Action (JCPOA) should go into effect sometime in mid-2016. Most analysts judge that substantial effort will need to be devoted to enforcing and maintaining the agreement and ensuring that Iran's nuclear programs remain peaceful afterward.

Overview

A majority of the international community has been at odds with Iran over its nuclear program because of its history of concealing its nuclear activities, the possible military nature of some of these activities, and its building of facilities in secret. Many of Iran's Arab neighbors, in addition to Israel, fear an Iranian nuclear bomb and could seek their own nuclear deterrent if Iran succeeds in acquiring nuclear weapons. Some countries in the Middle East may seek to duplicate Iran's nuclear capabilities, including uranium enrichment capabilities, although these efforts would likely be subject to international inspections.

Iran initially constructed in secret its gas centrifuge uranium enrichment program, including a large centrifuge plant at Natanz, and a heavy water production plant at Arak. The existence of these major facilities was revealed in 2002, and they were then placed under International Atomic Energy Agency (IAEA) inspections.

As part of settling international concern about its nuclear activities, Iran temporarily accepted more intrusive inspections by the U.N. nuclear watchdog. In 2006, Iran significantly reduced the inspection arrangements of the IAEA with its refusal to continue implementing the Additional Protocol to the Nuclear Non-Proliferation Treaty (NPT). This reversal prompted renewed concern that it could conduct significant nuclear activities in secret. The Protocol requires Iran to supply the IAEA with more detailed declarations of its nuclear activities and provide much greater access to nuclear sites than traditional safeguards. In response, the United Nations Security Council passed the first of several resolutions calling on Iran to suspend its activities and imposing sanctions on importing key goods to outfit its nuclear programs.

Amplifying worries about Iran's nuclear intentions, in September 2009, the United States, France, and Britain revealed the existence of a small, covert, and deeply buried uranium enrichment plant being built in Iran near the city of Qom. The United States suspected the facility could be used to quickly produce enough nuclear explosive material, or highly enriched uranium, for a nuclear weapon, in what is commonly called, "breakout." Iran denied any military nuclear intentions for the site and placed it under IAEA safeguards.

In November 2011, the IAEA released a report listing areas in which it had evidence of Iran's past and potentially ongoing work on nuclear weaponization and the development of nuclear warheads for missile delivery systems, or the so-called "possible military dimensions" (PMD) to its program. Iran and the IAEA agreed to a Roadmap alongside the JCPOA process, through which the IAEA will attempt to investigate the PMD matter and issue a full report of its findings by December 2015.

In November 2013, after a series of back channel talks between Iran and the United States, Iran and the P5+1 countries reached an interim agreement limiting Iran's nuclear programs. The Joint Plan of Action (JPOA) restricted the amount of enriched uranium Iran could produce, reduced the number of centrifuges and sites it could operate, lengthened the time to "break out"—or the amount of time it would take Iran to produce one significant quantity of weapon-grade uranium for a nuclear weapon—and opened its program to additional transparency. The agreement was intended to freeze Iran's nuclear progress while a longer term agreement to resolve the crisis could be negotiated.

In April 2015, a framework for a final deal was announced, and on July 14, 2015, a final deal was reached. The agreement will suspend and remove many key, stringent sanctions in exchange for a series of actions by Iran to scale back its nuclear program, address questions regarding past nuclear weapons related efforts and enhance inspectors' ability to monitor its activities. The deal has been criticized because it does not explicitly require Iran to satisfy the IAEA's concerns about past nuclear weapons work prior to the lifting of key sanctions. It also freezes Iran's centrifuge program for only 10 years, allowing Iran to increase the size of its gas centrifuge program, slowly during years 11 through 13 and relatively rapidly afterwards. Iran has stated it plans to build a substantially larger gas centrifuge program than it currently has, once restrictions expire 15 years after implementation. After year 15, if Iran expands its program as planned, breakout times are expected to be reduced to a few days or weeks, versus several months as of 2015.

Evolution

Iran's controversial nuclear program has evolved through at least seven phases.

Phase one: Beginnings 1950s–1960s

Iran first established its nuclear program in 1957, under Mohammad Reza Shah Pahlavi, with an agreement on nuclear cooperation with the United States under the Atoms for Peace program. In 1960, it purchased from the United States a small research reactor, which is located at the Tehran Nuclear Research Center. The reactor started in 1967. Iran signed the Nuclear Non-Proliferation Treaty in 1968, on the day it opened for signature. The United States provided highly enriched uranium fuel for the first several years of the reactor's operation. (In the early 1990s, Argentina took over providing low enriched uranium fuel).

Phase two: Ambitious options 1970s
The shah established the Atomic Energy Organization of Iran (AEOI) in 1974 and announced plans to build 20 nuclear power reactors for energy production. The United States, France, and West Germany subsequently sought lucrative power reactor deals. In 1974, Iran signed a contract with the German firm Kraftwerk Union (a subsidiary of Siemens) to build two reactors at Bushehr. It also purchased nearly 600 tons of uranium yellowcake from South Africa.

The shah wanted to keep open the option of developing nuclear weapons by seeking access to the full nuclear fuel cycle. The former head of AEOI, Akbar Etemad, revealed to *Le Figaro* in 2003 that he tasked a special research team with "giv[ing] the country access to all technologies, giving the political decision-makers the possibility of making the appropriate decision and doing so while time permitted them to build a bomb if that is what was required."

Iran attempted during the 1970s to develop laser enrichment technology and tried to acquire a plutonium reprocessing capability. Declassified U.S. government documents from 1974 to 1977 indicate that Iran's quest for a reprocessing capability was opposed by the United States during negotiations over sales of U.S. reactors to Iran. The United States also sought to deny the sale of a reprocessing facility from Germany to Iran. Washington eventually secured the right to the return and storage of spent reactor fuel from any reactors it built in Iran in a nuclear agreement concluded in 1978.

Phase three: Revolution, war and secret contacts 1979–1988
After the 1979 revolution, Iran suspended its nuclear program because of opposition to nuclear power by its new leader, Ayatollah Ruhollah Khomeini. Its nuclear cooperation with the United States ended with their rupture in bilateral relations. Construction on two

semi-finished reactors at Bushehr and plans for two reactors to be built by France at Ahvaz were scrapped. In 1982, Iran sought to resume work on the Bushehr reactors, partially due to the regime's recognition of the financial complexity of halting the commercial reactor project.

The devastating 1980–1988 Iran-Iraq War heavily influenced Ayatollah Khomeini's decision to re-start Iran's nuclear program. The war prompted leading political figures to call for Iran's development of a nuclear deterrent, demands that were bolstered by its fear of the United States and growing evidence of a covert Iraqi nuclear weapons program. A 2009 internal IAEA working document reports that in April 1984, then President Ali Khamenei announced to top Iranian officials that Khomeini had decided to launch a nuclear weapons program as the only way to secure the Islamic Revolution from the schemes of its enemies, especially the United States and Israel.

Iran began developing a gas centrifuge program in 1985, according to IAEA reports but realized that it needed foreign assistance to make progress on centrifuges. Iranians visited potential suppliers abroad in order to acquire and learn how to operate key centrifuge equipment. In 1987, Iran acquired key components from the A.Q. Khan network, a rogue nuclear supply network operating out of Pakistan's state-run nuclear weapons program. The components included:

- A starter kit for a gas centrifuge plant
- A set of technical drawings for a P-1 (Pakistani) centrifuge
- Samples of centrifuge components
- And instructions for enriching uranium to weapon-grade levels. (Weapon-grade uranium is the most desirable highly enriched uranium for fission nuclear weapons and is over 90 percent enriched.)

Phase four: Enrichment and procurement 1988–2002

Iran made deliberate, steady progress in its quest to achieve the full nuclear fuel cycle. It advanced its uranium mining infrastructure, uranium conversion capabilities, indigenous heavy water reactor and associated heavy water production plant, and uranium enrichment programs. In 1990, Iran and China signed a nuclear cooperation agreement. In 1991, Iran secretly imported from China one metric ton of uranium hexafluoride (UF_6), which it was obligated under its IAEA safeguards agreement to report to the Agency, but did not. Uranium hexafluoride is the feed gas for gas centrifuges and is difficult to make. Between 1994 and 1996, Iran also purchased from the A.Q. Khan network design drawings and components for 500 P-1 centrifuges, according to the IAEA. It received drawings for the more sophisticated P-2 centrifuge from the network in 1995 but claimed that it did not start work on the P-2 until 2002.

In early 1995, Russia began reconstructing one of the reactors at Bushehr, which had been badly damaged during the Iran-Iraq War. The United States persuaded Russia to halt its negotiations to sell Iran a centrifuge enrichment facility. Russian companies also provided technical assistance in designing a heavy water reactor that Iran was planning at Arak, but U.S. pressure succeeded in convincing Russia to halt cooperation on this venture in the late 1990s. Nonetheless, Iran received significant reactor and fuel design assistance from Russian entities. After years of delay, the Bushehr reactor was started in 2010 and will be under IAEA safeguards, with Russia providing the fuel and taking it back.

In 1999 and 2002, Iran conducted tests on centrifuges installed at Kalaye Electric Company, its secret centrifuge R&D facility, using the Chinese-supplied UF6. These tests constituted violations of Iran's safeguards agreements, or violations of Iran's verification requirements under the NPT. In 2001, again in secret, Iran began constructing a vast underground enrichment facility near the city of Natanz. In 2002, the National Council of Resistance of Iran held a press conference in Washington, D.C. to disclose secret nuclear activities taking place at Natanz and Arak, and revealed the names of entities and officials involved with the nuclear program. The Institute for Science and International Security (ISIS) located these sites and released satellite imagery of both Natanz and Arak in December 2002. ISIS identified Natanz as a gas centrifuge facility.

Iran continued its work on nuclear weapons capabilities throughout the 1990s and early 2000s, making substantial progress on learning to build crude nuclear explosives. It also made progress on miniaturizing nuclear warheads for deployment on ballistic missiles.

Phase five: Investigations, diplomacy and sanctions 2003-2009

The IAEA visited Iran's newly disclosed nuclear facilities in February 2003 following substantial international pressure for Iran to open its facilities to inspection. The Natanz above-ground pilot enrichment plant could hold 1,000 centrifuges, while its underground halls were equipped to hold 50,000. The agency also inspected the heavy water production facility at Arak.

Britain, France, and Germany, referred to as the EU-3, succeeded in the fall of 2003 in persuading Iran to verifiably suspend its uranium enrichment activities and implement the NPT's Additional Protocol. These two measures significantly strengthened the IAEA's ability to inspect Iran's nuclear program and ensure that it did not have secret nuclear sites. In 2004, Iran and the EU-3 signed the Paris Agreement, which extended the temporary suspension of Iran's nuclear activities, pending negotiations of long-term arrangements.

In secret, Iran suspended its work on nuclear weapons in 2003. Work on certain aspects of nuclear weapons development, however, may have continued afterwards, according to the IAEA.

Iran's suspension of its centrifuge activities lasted for three years, and then Iran restarted its gas centrifuge program and the manufacturing of centrifuges. It also resumed operations at the Isfahan uranium conversion facility that makes uranium hexafluoride. It stopped voluntarily implementing the Additional Protocol in 2006, and refused to answer satisfactorily the IAEA's questions about past or ongoing experimentation on nuclear weaponization and the development of nuclear warheads for missile delivery systems.

In mid-2009, the United States joined the EU-3 in diplomatic negotiations with Iran, after years of refusing to do so. These negotiations did not produce a breakthrough. In September 2009, the leaders of the United States, France, and Britain publicly revealed the existence of a secret uranium enrichment site being built underground near the holy city of Qom. The facility's revelation prompted concern that Iran intended to construct a potential breakout facility where it could quickly make weapon-grade uranium for a bomb. Iran agreed to place the facility under IAEA safeguards.

Against the backdrop of diplomatic negotiations, the U.N. Security Council passed four rounds of economic sanctions against Iran between 2006 and 2010 for its failure to suspend enrichment and cooperate adequately with the IAEA. The sanctions targeted entities and officials associated with the nuclear program, and Iran's illicit banking, shipping, and trading activities that supported its nuclear program.

Phase six: International tensions 2010–2012
Despite increasing sanctions, Iran refused to halt its enrichment program, and expanded work at Natanz and Fordo. It installed more advanced centrifuges capable of producing enriched uranium more quickly at Natanz and increased the level of enrichment at the Natanz pilot plant and the Fordo enrichment site. In 2010, Iran began enriching its 3.5 percent uranium to 20 percent at the Natanz pilot plant, purportedly for use in fueling the Tehran Research Reactor. Suspicions were that the underlying motivation was to learn to enrich even further, to 90 percent, or weapon-grade. In mid-2011, Iran started producing up to 20 percent enriched uranium at the Fordo plant, creating further tensions.

International efforts stalled in 2009 to broker a deal in which Iran would send most of its 3.5 percent enriched uranium out of the country, in return for 20 percent enriched fuel from abroad. This deal would have obviated the need for Iran to make 20 percent uranium. The United States proposed this deal as a way to build confidence in negotiations and extend the timeline of Iran acquiring the capability to make enough weapon-grade uranium for a nuclear weapon.

In mid-2010, most estimates put Iran six to 12 months away from being able to produce enough weapon-grade uranium to build a nuclear weapon, if it decided to do so. It would take longer to make the nuclear explosive itself. In late 2011, the IAEA released a report containing areas of outstanding concern it had over Iran's military nuclear programs based on evidence that Iran had worked on nuclear weaponization and the development of a missile delivery payload system. The IAEA and member states called on Iran to address the IAEA's concerns. Iran, however, dismissed the evidence as forgery or invention. The IAEA believed Iran acquired sufficient information to design and produce a workable implosion nuclear device based on highly enriched uranium as the fission fuel. A high-explosive implosion system developed by Iran could be contained within a payload container small enough to fit into the re-entry body chamber of the Shahab-3 missile. The IAEA did not believe that Iran had achieved the means to integrate a nuclear payload into the Shahab-3.

International discussion about the merits of a strike on Iran's nuclear facilities by Israel, the United States, or some combination of countries occurred, at odds with those favoring sanctions or engagement to induce Iran to change its apparent course. The United States and European Union introduced strong, targeted financial and oil sector sanctions against Iran in order to bring it to negotiate an end to the crisis and prevent it from building nuclear weapons. Iran's economy was under ever increasing pressure. Between 2009 and 2013, the United States and Iran held back channel talks over the possibility of nuclear negotiations. They soon reached a critical turning point.

Phase seven: International engagement 2013–2015
In 2013, the controversial presidency of Mahmoud Ahmadinejad concluded with the election of more moderate candidate Hassan Rouhani. After years of back channel talks with the United States and weathering stronger sanctions, Iran was more willing to negotiate by the time Rouhani took office. In November 2013, Iran and the P5+1 announced the Joint Plan of Action, an agreement that limited and froze portions of Iran's nuclear programs and introduced greater transparency while a longer term agreement could be negotiated. The parties later reached the Lausanne framework agreement on April 2, 2015 which spelled out several steps for a comprehensive agreement.

On July 14, 2015, Iran and the P5+1 announced the Joint Comprehensive Plan of Action (JCPOA). This agreement will suspend and finally remove key sanctions on Iran. In return, Iran will limit its nuclear program, address questions regarding past nuclear weapons related efforts, and enhance the ability of inspectors to detect undeclared nuclear work by implementing the Additional Protocol. The JCPOA also references a simultaneously developed Iran/IAEA Roadmap which will seek to resolve the possible military dimensions to Iran's nuclear programs by December 2015. The JCPOA will begin at Implementation Day, expected to be in mid-2016, after a series of steps by Iran to limit its nuclear programs and fulfill the IAEA Roadmap in order to remove sanctions.

Five key strengths of the JCPOA include:

1) Lengthening of Iran's "breakout time" from roughly one to two months as of late 2013 to seven to 12 months during the first ten years of the deal;

2) Limits on the growth of Iran's nuclear enrichment program for 10 years due to: maintenance of limited low-enriched uranium (LEU) stockpiles, no enrichment

over 3.67 percent allowed, and limits on advanced centrifuge development;

3) Blockage of the plutonium production pathway for 15 years through a re-design of Arak reactor, no production of heavy water, and no plutonium reprocessing allowed during this period;

4) Regulation of Iran's nuclear related imports for 10 years through a U.N. mandated procurement channel; and

5) Enhanced transparency and verification of Iran's nuclear program through its implementation of the Additional Protocol, a binding IAEA access provision to sites suspected of secret nuclear activities, and a parallel process for settling the IAEA's concerns about the possible military dimensions to Iran's nuclear program.

Five key weaknesses of the JCPOA include:

1) A quick return to shortened breakout timelines after year 10, decreasing from six months at year 13 to just days or weeks by year 15 as Iran deploys advanced centrifuges and caps on enrichment levels and LEU stockpiles come off, and possibly renewed international and regional concern over this future;

2) Limitations on Iran's nuclear related imports end at year 10 just as breakout timelines start to decrease, meaning Iran's nuclear program can import more freely a wide range of goods, making covert activities more difficult to observe. In addition, the procurement channel is complicated and is expected to be difficult to implement and enforce;

3) No intermediate penalties are outlined in the JCPOA for responding to minor problems or violations by Iran of its commitments. Most U.N. and national sanctions will be removed at the start of the agreement and only their full "snapback" is designated to deal with issues of noncompliance. This means that the deal would likely

be terminated by Iran over a P5+1 decision to escalate to snapback, thus the P5+1 may accept less than full compliance by Iran in order to avoid this. Leverage for ensuring Iranian compliance is thus far from certain;

4) The scope and manner of the investigation agreed to by the IAEA and Iran over PMD is unknown publicly. It is not known whether the PMD investigation will be as in-depth as past IAEA standards, including whether the IAEA will know enough to reach a conclusion on a past nuclear weapons program, or whether comprehensive inspections of suspect sites and interviews will occur;

5) Iran could deny the IAEA access to sites, information, or individuals, stating that they are military in nature, which could allow Iran to conduct covert nuclear activities. The P5+1 may tolerate refusals to cooperate or grant access, or even a weakened inspection arrangement, in order to keep the deal from collapsing. Iran is also not explicitly required to ratify the Additional Protocol by year 8, or Transition Day. It is unclear what happens if it does not, but the risk is that Iran could try to limit access and transparency past year 8 depending on the parties' interpretations and actions.

Factoids

- **Natanz**: The Natanz Fuel Enrichment Plant has had 9,156 IR-1 centrifuges enriching, and 15,420 IR-1 centrifuges installed since November 2013 when the interim agreement (JPOA) was agreed. Under the final deal (JCPOA), Iran will only be allowed to operate 5,060 IR-1 centrifuges at Natanz and enrich uranium up to 3.67 percent for 15 years.

- **Fordo:** The Fordo plant in Qom had 696 centrifuges that were enriching uranium to 19.75 percent up until the JPOA went into force in January 2014. Since then, the Fordo plant's centrifuges have enriched uranium only up to five percent. The plant was capable of housing 2,976 centrifuges until its expansion was frozen by the JPOA. Under the JCPOA, the Fordo facility will be converted into a nuclear, physics, and technology research center and will operate 1,044 IR-1 centrifuges in six cascades, which will not enrich uranium for a period of fifteen years. To many critics, one of the failings of the deal is that this plant was not shut down. After year 15 of the deal, it can resume enriching uranium in advanced centrifuges, up to 15 times more powerful than the current ones.

- **3.5 Percent LEU Inventory:** Based on data in the August 2015 IAEA Iran safeguards report, Iran has a total inventory of 7,845.4 kg of 3.5 percent LEU hexafluoride and the equivalent of another 4,304 kg of 3.5 percent LEU hexafluoride in various chemical forms at its Enriched UO_2 Powder Plant (EUPP). In total, Iran thus has the equivalent of 12,149 kg of 3.5 percent LEU hexafluoride. Under the JCPOA, Iran has agreed to remove or blend down all but 300 kg of this 3.5 percent LEU hexafluoride equivalent.

- **Decreasing 20 Percent LEU stockpile:** Iran has not been allowed to produce 19.75 percent LEU since the interim JPOA took effect and is required to downblend half this stock to 3.5 percent LEU and convert the other half to oxide form, a process it was still completing as of September 2015. While the Natanz Pilot Fuel Enrichment Plant produced 20 percent LEU, in total, Iran produced 202 kg of 19.75 percent enriched uranium since the beginning of operations in February 2010. In total, while it was producing 20 percent LEU, the Fordo facility produced 245.9 kg of near 20 percent LEU hexafluoride from 1,806 kg of 3.5 percent LEU hexafluoride. Almost all of this near 20 percent LEU is supposed to leave Iran under the long-term deal.

- **Breakout:** The capping of Iran's enrichment capabilities under the JCPOA will lengthen breakout timelines substantially, to roughly seven to 12 months. (The range reflects differences over whether it can redeploy its IR-2m centrifuges slated for dismantlement). After year 10, Iran will be allowed to deploy advanced centrifuges, reducing breakout timelines to about six months by year 13. After year 15 of the agreement, breakout timelines can reach as little as a few days with enrichment in advanced centrifuges and the removal of the cap on the 3.67 percent LEU and resumed production of near 20 percent LEU.

- **Plutonium:** The JCPOA prevents Iran from separating or reprocessing plutonium or acquiring heavy water reactors for 15 years. This provision intends to block Iran's plutonium pathway to nuclear weapons using its Arak reactor.

- **Possible military dimensions:** Iran will address PMD as mandated by the JCPOA under a separate arrangement with the IAEA called a Roadmap. The IAEA will issue a final report on the matter by December 2015. It will then seek a broader conclusion under the Additional Protocol procedures about the peacefulness of Iran's fissile material related nuclear activities.

- **Procurement:** The JCPOA establishes a procurement channel for Iran to legally acquire goods for its nuclear programs.

- **Site access:** The JCPOA creates a binding mechanism of 24 days to authorize access to a site in Iran sought by the IAEA due to reported suspicious activities.

- **More transparency:** Iran will provisionally implement the Additional Protocol and seek ratification at year 8 or Transition Day.

- **Sanctions:** Iran will receive relief from all United Nations nuclear related sanctions at Implementation Day of the JCPOA if it undertakes its nuclear measures. The European Union and United States will terminate or suspend their nuclear, financial, oil, and related sanctions against Iran at Implementation Day.

Individuals or organizations

- **Atomic Energy Council (AEC):** Iran's general nuclear policy is directed by the AEC, which was created by the same law that created the Atomic Energy Organization of Iran in 1974.

- **Atomic Energy Organization of Iran (AEOI):** The AEOI was established in 1974 to oversee Iran's civil nuclear program. It also oversaw Iran's clandestine nuclear activities.

- **Field for Expansion of Advanced Technologies' Deployment (FEDAT):** This is reportedly the most current name of the sector that worked on Iran's clandestine nuclear weapons-related activities.

- **Ministry of Defense:** The IAEA believes the ministry played an active role in the development of a nuclear payload for the Shahab-3 missile.

- **Supreme leader:** Ayatollah Ali Khamenei has ultimate say over Iran's nuclear program, and all major decisions on the nuclear issue require his approval.

- **Supreme National Security Council (SNSC):** The SNSC is concerned mainly with defense and national security policies. Key nuclear decisions are dominated by the supreme leader and a relatively small group of senior leaders and advisors, including those in the Supreme National Security Council.

Trendlines

- The size of Iran's sensitive nuclear programs will decrease substantially under the JCPOA.

- The JCPOA's fundamental goal is to ensure that Iran's nuclear program is peaceful even after its major nuclear limitations end. For 10 years, this agreement creates conditions that will make any serious effort by Iran to build nuclear weapons highly time consuming and vulnerable to detection. Whether the deal meets the goal of preventing Iran from building nuclear weapons in the long term is more doubtful. This uncertainty poses one of the more fundamental challenges to the agreement.

- There remain significant concerns that Iran will not address the IAEA's PMD concerns before Implementation Day and such a failure will impact negatively the success of the agreement. The investigation may not delve deeply into resolving the issues, and the PMD provisions may be left to interpretation by the IAEA and the P5+1 that is not clear to publics and many governments.

- A set of intrusive verification measures, such as the Additional Protocol, will remain in place after year 15 of the deal, but they may not be sufficient to stop Iran from obtaining nuclear weapons. Armed with a large centrifuge program, an Iranian attempt to break out to nuclear weapons would be detected—but probably not in time to take action to prevent it. Iran's breakout time could reach just days after year 15 of the agreement, based on its stated plans to grow its enrichment program to industrial levels.

- The JCPOA has many strengths that could temporarily resolve the Iranian nuclear issue due to the limits on Iran's nuclear growth, assuming it abides by the provisions. Implementation, however, may be difficult throughout its duration given past Iranian covert nuclear work, failures to abide by agreements, violations of trade controls and sanctions, and pushing against restrictions. Moreover, whether or not it succeeds after most limitations end will depend on Iran's actions that are difficult to predict. Therefore planning for and preventing shortened breakout timelines and a potentially renewed nuclear crisis after the deal ends is critical.

Why We Should Pursue Nuclear Power

Ernest Moniz

In the following viewpoint, Ernest Moniz argues that nuclear energy still has great potential worldwide. Despite major setbacks such as the Fukushima disaster in Japan, Moniz cites several reasons why nuclear energy is still a viable technology for investment. Compared to fossil fuels, nuclear power is much cleaner, and it is more reliable than renewable energy. New, small modular reactors (SMRs), though unproven, promise steady energy at less expense than large-scale reactors. Moniz concedes that waste management and weapons proliferation are still great concerns, but has faith that these problems all can be solved with proper ingenuity. Moniz is director of the Energy Initiative at MIT. He served as Undersecretary of the US Department of Energy in 1997–2001.

As you read, consider the following questions:

1. How does the author suggest nuclear accidents be averted in the future?
2. What are some of the advantages associated with small modular reactors?
3. Why is nuclear waste such a persistent problem?

In the years following the major accidents at Three Mile Island in 1979 and Chernobyl in 1986, nuclear power fell out of favor,

"Why we still need nuclear power," by Ernest Moniz, MIT Energy Initiative, November 2, 2011. Reprinted by permission.

and some countries applied the brakes to their nuclear programs. In the last decade, however, it began experiencing something of a renaissance. Concerns about climate change and air pollution, as well as growing demand for electricity, led many governments to reconsider their aversion to nuclear power, which emits little carbon dioxide and had built up an impressive safety and reliability record. Some countries reversed their phaseouts of nuclear power, some extended the lifetimes of existing reactors, and many developed plans for new ones. Today, roughly 60 nuclear plants are under construction worldwide, which will add about 60,000 megawatts of generating capacity—equivalent to a sixth of the world's current nuclear power capacity.

But the movement lost momentum in March, when a 9.0-magnitude earthquake and the massive tsunami it triggered devastated Japan's Fukushima nuclear power plant. Three reactors were severely damaged, suffering at least partial fuel meltdowns and releasing radiation at a level only a few times less than Chernobyl. The event caused widespread public doubts about the safety of nuclear power to resurface. Germany announced an accelerated shutdown of its nuclear reactors, with broad public support, and Japan made a similar declaration, perhaps with less conviction. Their decisions were made easier thanks to the fact that electricity demand has flagged during the world-wide economic slowdown and the fact that global regulation to limit climate change seems less imminent now than it did a decade ago. In the United States, an already slow approach to new nuclear plants slowed even further in the face of an unanticipated abundance of natural gas.

It would be a mistake, however, to let Fukushima cause governments to abandon nuclear power and its benefits. Electricity generation emits more carbon dioxide in the United States than does transportation or industry, and nuclear power is the largest source of carbon-free electricity in the country. Nuclear power generation is also relatively cheap, costing less than two cents per kilowatt-hour for operations, maintenance, and fuel. Even after the Fukushima disaster, China, which accounts for about 40 percent of current nuclear power plant construction, and India, Russia, and South Korea, which together account for another 40 percent, show no signs of backing away from their pushes for nuclear power.

Nuclear power's track record of providing clean and reliable electricity compares favorably with other energy sources. Low natural gas prices, mostly the result of newly accessible shale gas, have brightened the prospects that efficient gas-burning power plants could cut emissions of carbon dioxide and other pollutants relatively quickly by displacing old, inefficient coal plants, but the historical volatility of natural gas prices has made utility companies wary of putting all their eggs in that basket. Besides, in the long run, burning natural gas would still release too much carbon dioxide. Wind and solar power are becoming increasingly widespread, but their intermittent and variable supply make them poorly suited for large-scale use in the absence of an affordable way to store electricity. Hydropower, meanwhile, has very limited prospects for expansion in the United States because of environmental concerns and the small number of potential sites.

Still, nuclear power faces a number of challenges in terms of safety, construction costs, waste management, and weapons proliferation. After Fukushima, the U.S. Nuclear Regulatory Commission, an independent federal agency that licenses nuclear reactors, reviewed the industry's regulatory requirements, operating procedures, emergency response plans, safety design requirements, and spent-fuel management. The NRC will almost certainly implement a number of the resulting recommendations, and the cost of doing business with nuclear energy in the United States will inevitably go up. Those plants that are approaching the end of their initial 40-year license period, and that lack certain modern safety features, will face additional scrutiny in having their licenses extended.

At the same time, new reactors under construction in Finland and France have gone billions of dollars over budget, casting doubt on the affordability of nuclear power plants. Public concern about radioactive waste is also hindering nuclear power, and no country yet has a functioning system for disposing of it. In fact, the U.S. government is paying billions of dollars in damages to utility companies for failing to meet its obligations to remove spent fuel from reactor sites. Some observers are also concerned that the spread of civilian nuclear energy infrastructure could lead to the proliferation of nuclear weapons—a problem exemplified by Iran's uranium-enrichment program.

If the benefits of nuclear power are to be realized in the United States, each of these hurdles must be overcome. When it comes to safety, the design requirements for nuclear reactors must be reexamined in light of up-to-date analyses of plausible accidents. As for cost, the government and the private sector need to advance new designs that lower the financial risk of constructing nuclear power plants. The country must also replace its broken nuclear waste management system with a more adaptive one that safely disposes of waste and stores it for centuries. Only then can the public's trust be earned.

Safer and Cheaper

The tsunami that hit Japan in March marked the first time that an external event led to a major release of radioactivity from a nuclear power plant. The 14-meter-high wave was more than twice the height that Fukushima was designed to withstand, and it left the flooded plant cut off from external logistical support and from its power supply, which is needed to cool the reactor and pools of spent fuel. Such natural disasters, although infrequent, should have been planned for in the reactor's design: the Pacific Ring of Fire has seen a dozen earth- quakes in the 8.5 to 9.5 range in the last hundred years, and Japan has the most recorded tsunamis in the world, with waves sometimes reaching 30 meters high. Just four years ago, the world's largest nuclear generating station, Kashiwazaki-Kariwa, was shut down by an earthquake that shook the plant beyond what it was designed to handle, and three of the seven reactors there remain idle today.

The Fukushima disaster will cause nuclear regulators everywhere to reconsider safety requirements—in particular, those specifying which accidents plants must be designed to withstand. In the 40 years since the first Fukushima reactor was commissioned, seismology and the science of flood hazards have made tremendous progress, drawing on advances in sensors, modeling, and other new capabilities. This new knowledge needs to be brought to bear not only when designing new power plants but also when revisiting the requirements at older plants, as was happening at Fukushima before the tsunami. Outdated safety requirements should not be kept in place. In the United States, the NRC's review led to a recommendation that nuclear power plant operators reevaluate seismic and flood hazards every ten years and alter the design of the plants and their operating procedures as appropriate. With few exceptions, the needed upgrades are likely to be modest, but such a step would help ensure that the designs of plants reflect up-to-date information.

The NRC also proposed regulations that would require nuclear power stations to have systems in place to allow them to remain safe if cut off from outside power and access for up to three days. It issued other recommendations addressing issues such as the removal of combustible gas and the monitoring of spent-fuel storage pools. These proposals do not mean that the NRC lacks confidence in the safety of U.S. nuclear reactors; their track record of running 90 percent of the time is an indicator of good safety performance and extraordinary when compared with other methods of electricity generation. Nevertheless, the incident at Fukushima clearly calls for additional regulatory requirements, and the NRC's recommendations should be put in place as soon as is feasible.

New regulations will inevitably increase the costs of nuclear power, and nuclear power plants, with a price tag of around $6–$10 billion each, are already much more expensive to build than are plants powered by fossil fuels. Not only are their capital costs inherently high; their longer construction times mean that utility companies accumulate substantial financing charges before they can sell any electricity. In an attempt to realize economies of scale, some utilities have turned to building even larger reactors, building ones that produce as much as 1,600 megawatts, instead of the typical 1,000 megawatts. This pushes up the projects' cost and amplifies the consequences of mistakes during construction.

All this can make nuclear power plants seem like risky investments, which in turn raises investors' demands on return and the cost of borrowing money to finance the projects. Yet nuclear power enjoys low operating costs, which can make it competitive on the basis of the electricity price needed to recover the capital investment over a plant's lifetime. And if governments eventually cap carbon dioxide emissions through either an emissions charge or a regulatory requirement, as they are likely to do in the next decade or so, then nuclear energy will be more attractive relative to fossil fuels.

In the United States, there is still a great deal of uncertainty over the cost of new nuclear power plants. It has been almost 40 years since the last new nuclear power plant was ordered. The Tennessee Valley Authority, a federally owned corporation, is currently finishing construction of the Watts Bar Unit 2 reactor, in eastern Tennessee, which was started long ago, and it has plans to complete another, Bellefonte Unit 1, in Hollywood, Alabama. The first new nuclear plants of next-generation design are likely to be built in Georgia by the Southern Company, pending the NRC's approval. Scheduled for completion in 2016, the proposed project entails two reactors totaling 2,200 megawatts at an estimated cost of $14 billion. It will take advantage of substantial subsidies (loan guarantees, production tax credits, and the reimbursement of costs caused by regulatory delay) that were put forward in the 2005 Energy Policy Act to kick-start the construction of new nuclear plants. Even after Fukushima, Congress and the White House appear to still be committed to this assistance program. The success or failure of these construction projects in avoiding delays and cost overruns will help determine the future of nuclear power in the United States.

A Smaller Solution

The safety and capital cost challenges involved with traditional nuclear power plants may be considerable, but a new class of reactors in the development stage holds promise for addressing them. These reactors, called small modular reactors (SMRs), produce anywhere from ten to 300 megawatts, rather than the 1,000 megawatts produced by a typical reactor. An entire reactor, or at least most of it, can be built in a factory and shipped to a site for assembly, where several reactors can be installed together to compose a larger nuclear power station. SMRs have attractive safety features, too. Their design often incorporates natural cooling features that can continue to function in the absence of external power, and the underground placement of the reactors and the spent-fuel storage pools is more secure.

Since SMRrs are smaller than conventional nuclear plants, the construction costs for individual projects are more manageable, and thus the financing terms may be more favorable. And because they are factory-assembled, the on-site construction time is shorter. The utility company can build up its nuclear power capacity step by step, adding additional reactors as needed, which means that it can generate revenue from electricity sales sooner. This helps not only the plant owner but also customers, who are increasingly being asked to pay higher rates today to fund tomorrow's plants.

The assembly-line-like production of SMRs should lower their cost, too. Rather than chasing elusive economies of scale by building larger projects, SMR vendors can take advantage of the economies of manufacturing: a skilled permanent work force, quality control, and continuous improvement in reactors' design and manufacturing. Even though the intrinsic price per megawatt for SMRs may be higher than that for a large-scale reactor, the final cost per megawatt might be lower thanks to more favorable financing terms and shorter construction times—a proposition

The Future of Nuclear Power

Today, nuclear energy supplies almost 11.5% of global electricity needs in 31 countries. Sixteen countries depend on nuclear power for at least a quarter of their electricity. Leading five nuclear generating countries—by rank, the United States, France, Russia, South Korea and China—generated over two-thirds (69 percent in 2014) of the world's nuclear electricity in 2014. The U.S. and France account for half of global nuclear generation, and France produces half of the European Union's nuclear output. About 60 further nuclear power reactors are under construction, equivalent to 16% of existing capacity, while over 160 are firmly planned and equivalent to nearly half of present capacity.

One main advantage of nuclear energy is that the fuel forms a low proportion of nuclear power cost which in turn brings in the advantage of low operational cost of the power plants...However, nuclear energy sector suffers from one of the greatest disadvantages, that is, ageing plants with most of the world's nuclear reactors built in the 1970s and 1980s.

There's been no diminution in the intensity of the debate about the role of nuclear power in tomorrow's low-carbon world. Indeed, it seems to become more intense by the day. Curbing climate-changing emissions has become a common goal of most governments and major energy corporations and nuclear power offers an abundant source of carbon-free energy. When well-operated, nuclear plants also have the lowest down-time of any other kind of power. However, the future for the sector is not that smooth and lots of things need to be done on the technological front and that too very fast. [...]

"Nuclear Power Around the World," by Shannon Andrade, October 7, 2016.

that will have to be tested. The feasibility of SMRs needs to be demonstrated, and the government will almost certainly need to share some of the risk to get this done.

No SMR design has yet been licensed by the NRC. This is a time-consuming process for any new nuclear technology, and it will be especially so for those SMR designs that represent significant departures from the NRC's experience. Only after SMRs are licensed and built will their true cost be clear. The catch, however, is that the economies of manufacturing can be realized and understood only if there is a reliable stream of orders to keep the manufacturing lines busy turning out the same design. In order for that to happen, the U.S. government will have to figure out how to incubate early movers while not locking in one technology prematurely.

With the U.S. federal budget under tremendous pressure, it is hard to imagine taxpayers funding demonstrations of a new nuclear technology. But if the United States takes a hiatus from creating new clean-energy options—be it SMRs, renewable energy, advanced batteries, or carbon capture and sequestration—Americans will look back in ten years with regret. There will be fewer economically viable options for meeting the United States' energy and environmental needs, and the country will be less competitive in the global technology market.

Waste Basket Case

If nuclear energy is to enjoy a sustained renaissance, the challenge of managing nuclear waste for thousands of years must be met. Nuclear energy is generated by splitting uranium, leaving behind dangerous radioactive products, such as cesium and strontium that must be isolated for centuries. The process also produces transuranic elements, such as plutonium, which are heavier than uranium, do not occur in nature, and must be isolated for millennia. There is an alternative to disposing of transuranic elements: they can be separated from the reactor fuel every few years and then recycled into new nuclear reactor fuel as an additional energy source. The downside, however, is that this process is complex and expensive, and it poses a proliferation risk since plutonium can be used in nuclear weapons. The debate over the merits of recycling transuranic elements has yet to be resolved.

What is not disputed is that most nuclear waste needs to be isolated deep underground. The scientific community has supported this method for decades, but finding sites for the needed facilities has proved difficult. In the United States, Congress adopted a prescriptive approach, legislating both a single site, at

Yucca Mountain, in Nevada, and a specific schedule for burying spent fuel underground. The massive project was to be paid for by a nuclear waste fund into which nuclear power utilities contribute about $750 million each year. But the strategy backfired, and the program is in a shambles. Nevada pushed back, and the schedule slipped by two decades, which meant that the government had to pay court-ordered damages to the utility companies. In 2009, the Obama administration announced that it was canceling the Yucca Mountain project altogether, leaving no alternative in place for the disposal of radioactive waste from nuclear power plants. The Nuclear Waste Fund has reached $25 billion but has no disposal program to support.

Fukushima awakened the American public and members of Congress to the problem of the accumulation of radioactive spent fuel in cooling pools at reactor sites. The original plan had been to allow the spent fuel to cool for about five years, after which it would be either disposed of underground or partly recycled. Now, the spent nuclear fuel has nowhere to go. Many utilities have moved some of the spent fuel out of the pools and into dry storage facilities built on site, which the NRC has judged safe for a century or so. The dry storage facilities at Fukushima were not compromised by the earthquake and tsunami, a sharp contrast to the problems that arose with the spent-fuel pools when cooling could not be maintained. To deal with the immediate problem of waste building up in reactor pools, Congress should allow the Nuclear Waste Fund to be used for moving the spent fuel accumulating in pools into dry-cask storage units nearby. But such an incremental step should not substitute for a comprehensive approach to waste management.

Instead of being stored near reactors, spent fuel should eventually be kept in dry casks at a small number of consolidated sites set up by the government where the fuel could stay for a century. This approach has several advantages. The additional cooling time would provide the Department of Energy, or some other organization, with more flexibility in designing a geological repository. The government would no longer have to pay utilities for not meeting the mandated schedule, and communities near reactors would be reassured that spent fuel has a place to go. At each site, the aging fuel would be monitored, so that any problems that arose could be addressed. The storage facilities would keep Washington's options open as the debate over whether spent fuel is waste or a resource works itself out. These sites should be paid for by the Nuclear Waste Fund, a change that would require congressional approval.

At the same time, Washington must find an alternative to Yucca Mountain for storing nuclear waste in the long run. As it does so, it must adopt a more adaptive and flexible approach than it did last time, holding early negotiations with local communities, Native American tribes, and states. Sweden upgraded its waste disposal program with just such a consensus-based process, and for a dozen years the U.S. Department of Energy has operated a geological repository for trans-uranic waste near Carlsbad, New Mexico, with strong community support. The government should also investigate new approaches to disposal. For example, it might make sense to separate out the long-living transuranic elements in nuclear reactor waste, which constitute a nasty but very small package, and dispose of them in a miles-deep borehole, while placing the shorter-living materials in repositories closer to the surface. Given the sustained challenge of waste management, an overhaul to the existing program should include the establishment of a new federally chartered organization that is a step or two removed from the short-term political calculus.

Another break from the past would be to manage civilian nuclear waste separately from military nuclear waste. In 1985, the government elected to comingle defense and civilian waste in a single geological repository. This made sense at the time, since the planners assumed that Yucca Mountain would be available for storing both types. But now, it looks as though it will be many years before a large-scale repository opens. Today, it makes more sense to put plans for storing military waste on a separate, faster track, since that process is less daunting than coming up with a solution to civilian waste. To begin with, there is simply much less military waste, and the volume will hardly grow in the future. Moreover, most of the military waste already has the uranium and plutonium separated out from the spent fuel, since the aim was to produce nuclear weapons material. Thus, what is left is definitely waste, not a resource.

Fast-tracking a defense waste program would allow the federal government to meet its obligations to states that host nuclear weapons facilities, from which it has agreed to remove radioactive waste. It would also make the finances of waste storage much clearer, since the nuclear utility companies pay for their waste management, whereas Congress has to approve payments for defense waste. And assuming a defense waste repository were established first, the experience gained operating it would be highly valuable when it comes time to establish a civilian one.

The United States' dysfunctional nuclear waste management system has an unfortunate international side effect: it limits the options for preventing other countries from using nuclear power infrastructure to produce nuclear weapons. If countries such as Iran are able to enrich uranium to make new reactor fuel and separate out the plutonium to recover its energy value, they then have access to the relevant technology and material for a weapons program. Safeguards agreements with the International Atomic Energy Agency are intended to make sure that civilian programs do not spill over into military ones, but the agency has only a limited ability to address clandestine programs.

Developing enrichment or separation facilities is expensive and unlikely to make economic sense for countries with small nuclear power programs. What these countries care about most is an assured supply of reactor fuel and a way to alleviate the burden of waste management. One promising scheme to keep fissile material out of the hands of would-be proliferators involves returning nuclear waste to the fuel-supplying country (or a third country). In effect, nuclear fuel could be leased to produce electricity. The country supplying the fuel would treat the returned spent fuel as it does its own, disposing of it directly or reprocessing it. In most cases, the amount of additional waste would be small in comparison to what that country is already handling. In return for giving up the possibility of reprocessing fuel and thus separating out weapons-grade material, the country using the fuel would free itself from the challenges of managing nuclear waste.

The United States already runs a similar program on a smaller scale, having provided fuel, often highly enriched uranium, to about 30 countries for small research reactors. But with no functioning commercial waste management system in place, the program cannot be extended to accommodate waste from commercial reactors. Instead, Washington is trying to use diplomacy to impose constraints on a country-by- country basis, in the futile hope that countries will agree to give up enrichment and reprocessing in exchange for nuclear cooperation with the United States. This ad hoc approach might have worked when the United States was the dominant supplier of nuclear technology and fuel, but it no longer is, and other major suppliers, such as France and Russia, appear uninterested in imposing such restrictions on commercial transactions. Putting together a coherent waste management program would give the United States a leg to stand on when it comes to setting up a proliferation-resistant international fuel-cycle program.

Now or Never

As greenhouse gases accumulate in the atmosphere, finding ways to generate power cleanly, affordably, and reliably is becoming an even more pressing imperative. Nuclear power is not a silver bullet, but it is a partial solution that has proved workable on a large scale. Countries will need to pursue a combination of strategies to cut emissions, including reining in energy demand, replacing coal power plants with cleaner natural gas plants, and investing in new technologies such as renewable energy and carbon capture and sequestration. The government's role should be to help provide the private sector with a well-understood set of options, including nuclear power—not to prescribe a desired market share for any specific technology.

The United States must take a number of decisions to maintain and advance the option of nuclear energy. The NRC's initial reaction to the safety lessons of Fukushima must be translated into action; the public needs to be convinced that nuclear power is safe. Washington should stick to its plan of offering limited assistance for building several new nuclear reactors in this decade, sharing the lessons learned across the industry. It should step up its support for new technology, such as SMRs and advanced computer-modeling tools. And when it comes to waste management, the government needs to overhaul the current system and get serious about long-term storage. Local concerns about nuclear waste facilities are not going to magically disappear; they need to be addressed with a more adaptive, collaborative, and transparent waste program.

These are not easy steps, and none of them will happen overnight. But each is needed to reduce uncertainty for the public, the energy companies, and investors. A more productive approach to developing nuclear power—and confronting the mounting risks of climate change—is long overdue. Further delay will only raise the stakes.

The Drawbacks of Nuclear Power

Mark Diesendorf

In the following viewpoint, Mark Diesendorf provides several reasons why the cons of nuclear energy outweigh the pros. As uranium ore supplies dwindle, mining will become more carbon intensive, thus negating nuclear energy's climate benefits. Since nuclear weapons programs emerge from civil nuclear technology, more nuclear power means increased probability a nuclear weapon will be detonated. Finally, new plants are slow to come online and often run over budget. For these reasons, investment in renewable technologies should be encouraged. Countries such as Denmark and Germany are leading the way with ambitious projections for renewable energy. Diesendorf is associate professor of interdisciplinary environmental studies at the University of New South Wales, Australia. His latest book is Sustainable Energy Solutions for Climate Change *(2014).*

As you read, consider the following questions:

1. Why is nuclear energy less carbon neutral than advocates claim?
2. What major problems with nuclear power does this article specify?
3. Are wind and solar energy reliable, according to the author? If not, are there easy solutions to problems with these power sources?

T he case for expanding nuclear energy is based on myths about its status, greenhouse gas emissions, proliferation, accidents, wastes and economics. Let's take each in turn.

Status

Nuclear is not, and has never been, a major energy force. Global annual nuclear energy generation peaked in 2006. Meanwhile its percentage contribution to global electricity generation has declined from its historic peak in 1993 of 17% to about 10% today. The only countries with significant growth are China, India, Russia and South Korea. In the rest of the world, retirements of ageing reactors are likely to outweigh new builds.

Greenhouse emissions

Nuclear advocates are fond of claiming that nuclear energy has negligible greenhouse gas emissions and hence must play an important role in mitigating climate change. However, the greenhouse case for new nuclear power stations is flawed.

In a study published in 2008, nuclear physicist and nuclear energy supporter Manfred Lenzen compared life-cycle emissions from several types of power station. For nuclear energy based on mining high-grade uranium ore, he found average emissions of 60 grams of CO_2 per kilowatt hour of electricity generation, compared with 10–20 g per kWh for wind and 500–600 g per kWh for gas. Now comes the part that most nuclear proponents try to ignore.

The world has, at most, a few decades of high-grade uranium ore reserves left. As ore grades inevitably decline, more diesel fuel is needed to mine and mill the uranium, and so the resulting CO_2 emissions rise. Lenzen calculated the life-cycle emissions of a nuclear power station running on low-grade uranium ore to be 131 g per kWh.

This is unacceptable in terms of climate science, especially given that Lenzen's assumptions favoured nuclear energy. Mining in remote locations will be one of the last industries to transition to low-carbon fuels, so new nuclear reactors will inevitably become significant greenhouse gas emitters over their lifetimes.

The next generation of reactors

Some generation IV reactors are potentially lower in life-cycle greenhouse gas emissions, but these are not yet commercially available.

All are likely to be even more expensive than conventional reactors. The fast breeder reactor is even more complex, dangerous, expensive and conducive to weapons proliferation than conventional nuclear reactors. Despite several decades of expensive pilot and demonstration plants, fast breeders have not been successfully commercialised, and may never be.

Advocates try to justify the integral fast reactor and the thorium reactor on the fallacious grounds that they cannot be used to produce nuclear weapons explosives. However, if not operated according to the rules, the integral fast reactor can actually make it easier to extract weapons-grade plutonium and hence make bombs. To be useful as a nuclear fuel, thorium must first be converted to uranium-233, which can be fissioned either in a nuclear reactor or an atomic bomb, as the United States has demonstrated.

The small modular reactor (SMR) has been a dream of the nuclear industry for decades, amid hopes that future mass production could make its electricity cheaper than from existing large reactors. However, offsetting this is the economy of scale of large reactors. The Union of Concerned Scientists, which is not anti-nuclear, has serious safety and security concerns about SMRs.

Weapons proliferation

Nuclear proponents dismiss the danger that civil nuclear energy will drive the development of nuclear weapons, by saying that the nuclear industry is now under strong international oversight. This ignores the harsh reality that India, Pakistan, North Korea and South Africa have all used civil nuclear energy to help build their nuclear weapons. Furthermore, Australia, Argentina, Brazil, Iran,

Libya, South Korea and Taiwan all used civil nuclear energy to cloak their commencement of nuclear weapons programs, although fortunately all except Iran have now discontinued them.

Thus nuclear energy contributes to the number of countries with nuclear weapons, or the capacity to build them, and hence increases the probability of nuclear war.

Accidents

Analyses of the damage done by major nuclear accidents, such as Chernobyl in 1986 and Fukushima in 2011, should properly consider not just the short-term deaths from acute radiation syndrome, but also the cancers that appear over the ensuring decades, and which represent the major contribution to death and disabilities from these incidents.

Estimates of future Chernobyl deaths by reputable impartial authors range from 16,000 by the International Centre for Research on Cancer, to 93,000 by an international group of medical researchers.

Four years after Fukushima, the plant is still leaking radiation, while a reported 120,000 people remain displaced and Japanese taxpayers face a bill that could run to hundreds of billions of dollars.

Economics

Proponents often cherry-pick highly optimistic projections of the future cost of nuclear energy. However, past and present experience suggests that such projections have little basis in reality. Apart from the Generation IV reactors, which are not commercially available and hence cannot be costed credibly, all of the much-touted current (Generation III+) power reactors under construction (none is operating) are behind schedule and over budget.

In Finland, Olkiluoto-3 is nearly a decade behind schedule and nearly three times its budgeted cost; in France, Flamanville-3 is five years behind schedule and double budgeted cost; in Georgia, USA, Vogtle is three years behind schedule and about US$700 million over budget. Britain's proposed Hinkley Point C will receive a guaranteed inflation-linked price for electricity over 35 years, starting at about US$180 per megawatt hour—double the typical wholesale price of electricity in the UK. It will also receive a loan guarantee of about US$20 billion and insurance backed by the British taxpayer. It's doubtful whether any nuclear power station has ever been built without huge subsidies.

Nuclear waste vs renewable energy

High-level nuclear wastes will have to be safeguarded for 100,000 years or more, far exceeding the lifetime of any human institution.

Meanwhile, Denmark is moving to 100% renewable electricity by 2035, and Germany to at least 80% by 2050. Two German states are already at 100% net renewable energy and South Australia is nudging 40%. Hourly computer simulations of the National Electricity Market suggest that it too could be operated on 100% renewables, purely by scaling up commercially available technologies.

The variability of wind and solar power can be managed with mixes of different renewable energy technologies, at geographically dispersed locations to smooth out the supply. Why would we need to bother with nuclear?

CHAPTER 2

Exploring the Politics of Nuclear Energy

History and Creation of Nuclear Energy

Energy Future

In the following viewpoint, Energy Future traces the history and development of nuclear energy. During World War II, the United States and England doubled-down on secret nuclear research in a race to beat Nazi Germany to the bomb. The allies were successful with the Manhattan Project, which developed the first viable nuclear weapon. The United States used these against Japan, ending the war with horrific devastation and civilian casualties. Eisenhower's Atoms for Peace program and the Atomic Energy Commission (AEC) were soon established, and within a few years, the first commercial nuclear reactor was built in Shippingport, Pennsylvania. The remainder of this viewpoint explores present and future nuclear power generation in depth.

As you read, consider the following questions:

1. Which states rely on nuclear power for a high proportion of their electricity needs?
2. What are the two types of nuclear reactors? Which is a more commonly used design?
3. Who are some of the companies involved in the nuclear power industry, and how do they differ?

"Nuclear Resources," The Future of Energy, November 11, 2010. http://energyfuture. wikidot.com/nuclear-resources. Licensed under CC BY-SA 3.0.

Nuclear Resources

History of Nuclear Power

Nuclear power as a sustainable source of power in the United States is an extremely viable and also extremely controversial subject matter. For these main reasons it is important to know the history associated with the fuel source in order to enhance output; reduce waste; and, most importantly, improve safety standards.

Creation of Nuclear Power

Before the turn of the twentieth century scientists were beginning to discover that atoms contained large amounts of energy. Ancient Greek philosophers developed the idea that matter is composed of invisible particles called atoms. The word atom comes from the Greek word, atomos, meaning indivisible.

The science of atomic radiation was mainly discovered and developed between the years of 1895 to 1945. The majority of the discoveries leading to nuclear fission and power were implemented between 1939 and 1945. The main reason for the high focus on this science was due to World War II. Within the United States, much of the research began and was developed around the Manhattan Project. The Manhattan Project was a project implemented during wartime for the research and development of the first atomic bombs. The committee informally began in 1939 with letters from Albert Einstein and Leó Szilárd to President Roosevelt concerning the threat of Nazi Germany implementing nuclear weapons against the Allies. In 1942 the US Army took over the Manhattan Project. This greatly impaired the information flow to Britain who was also working on the weapon. Eventually, Roosevelt and Churchill came to an agreement in Quebec in August 1943, in which the British handed over all their reports and research to the United States. This collaboration of information eventually led to the atomic bomb.

The nuclear bomb was a precursor of many new improvements to come. Not only as a weapon or threat but as a power source that brings simplicity and ingenuity to a rapidly growing United States nation. After the atomic bombs were dropped and the war was over, the United States government began the encouragement of utilizing nuclear energy for peaceful civilian purposes. President Roosevelt issued the "Atoms for Peace" program; with this motivation, Congress created the Atomic Energy Commission (AEC).

The AEC authorized the construction of Experimental Breeder Reactor I in Idaho. The reactor was a success and generated its first electricity on December 20th, 1951. However, this reactor was not commercially viable. The first commercially viable nuclear reactor was located in Shippingport, Pennsylvania, in 1957. After the success of the Shippingport reactor, private industry began to become more involved.

The nuclear power began a craze in the nation and nuclear power plants began to flourish throughout the United States. Mainly throughout the eastern coast of the nation.

Between 1975 and 78 the amount of reactors licensed dropped dramatically due to the rising constructions times and falling fossil fuel prices made nuclear power very unattractive.

Three Mile Island Incident

The Three Mile Island Incident was a great turning point in nuclear power throughout the United States. At 6:56 A.M. on March 28th, 1979 an emergency state was ordered for the Three Mile Island Nuclear Power Plant. This emergency arose due to a stuck open pilot-operated relief valve in the primary system along with human error. This was a contributing factor in the declining construction of nuclear power plants in the United States. There was an incline in construction every year up until 1979. However, along with the low fuel costs and threats of overcapacity, construction from 1980-present of nuclear power plants has been declining. At the time of the Three Mile Island incident there were 129 nuclear power plants approved, of those, only 53 were completed. This incident also led to greater opposition to the industry along with lengthened construction intervals due to higher safety regulations.

Current U.S. Nuclear Power

There are currently 65 nuclear power plants in the United States containing a total of 104 reactors. This is approximately 1.6 reactors per power plant. 35 reactors are Boiling Water Reactors (BWR), and 69 are Pressurized Water Reactors (PWR). Of the 35 BWR, 14 plants have one reactor, 9 have two reactors, and 1 has three reactors. Of the 69 PWR, 15 plants have one reactor, 24 have two reactors and 2 have three reactors. There are 31 states with operating nuclear reactors:

There are also seven states in which nuclear power makes up for the largest percentage of their electricity generated.

STATE	PERCENT OF ELECTRICITY GENERATED FROM NUCLEAR
Vermont	72.3
New Jersey	55.1
Connecticut	53.4
South Carolina	52.0
Illinois	48.7
New Hampshire	44.1
Virginia	39.6

Current Plants

The Palo Verde plant, in Arizona, is the biggest plant in the United States, it contains 3 reactors with individual reactors being able to produce 1,311 MW, 1,314 MW and 1,317 MW for a total of 3,942 MW.

The smallest plant in operation in the United States is the Fort Calhoun plant in Nebraska which contains 1 reactor capable of 482 MW.

The last nuclear power plant was Watts Bar 1 built in June of 1996 in Tennessee, which produces 1,123 MW.

Our nation's oldest operating nuclear power plant is Oyster Creek in New Jersey which has an operating license issued April 1969.

How It Works—Nuclear Reactors

Fission

This occurs when a large nucleus with fissile properties absorbs a neutron. The heavy nucleus can split into two or more lighter nuclei, releasing fission products like gamma radiation, free neutrons, and kinetic energy. A portion of these neutrons may be absorbed by other fissile atoms and trigger further fission events, this cycle will continue to occur and is known as a nuclear chain reaction. The reaction can be controlled by using neutron poisons. These will absorb excess neutrons, and neutron moderators, which reduces the velocity of fast neutrons. This increase or decrease of the rate of fission has a corresponding effect on the energy output of the reactor.

Heat Generation

The reactor is able to generate heat in a number of different ways. The most common way is the kinetic energy of the fission products being converted to thermal energy when their nuclei collide with other atoms. Other ways involve gamma rays that are produced during fission being absorbed and being converted to heat. Radioactive decay also produces heat. This heat source is able to remain some time after the reactor is no longer operating.

The heat generation from a reactor is much higher than any comparable source. A kilogram of U-235 converted contains approximately three million times the energy of a kilogram of coal burned conventionally (7.2×10^{13} joules per kilogram of uranium-235 versus 2.4×10^{7} joules per kilogram of coal).

Cooling

The coolant for a nuclear reactor is typically water but it can range to things such as a gas or a liquid metal. Whatever the coolant, it is circulated past the reactor core to absorb heat. The heat is carried away from the reactor and is then used to generate steam.

The next step in the process varies depending upon whether it is a pressurized water reactor or a boiling water reactor. Both of which will be addressed a little later.

Reactivity control

The power output of the reactor is controlled by controlling how many neutrons are able to create more fissions. This can be done by several different methods. Control rods are the most common method for this. They are made up of nuclear poisons that are designed to absorb neutrons. Absorbing more neutrons in a control rod means that there are fewer neutrons available to cause fission, so pushing the control rod deeper into the reactor will reduce its power output, and extracting the control rod will increase it.

In some reactors the coolant can also act as a moderator for neutrons. It will increase the power of the reactor by causing the fast neutrons that are released from fission to lose energy and become thermal neutrons. The thermal neutrons are more likely to cause fission, so more neutron moderation means more power output from the reactors.

Coolants can also acts as a poison by absorbing neutrons in the same way that the control rods do. In these reactors power output can either be decreased or increased based on the temperature. When heated it will make the coolant a less dense poison and vice-versa.

Electrical Power Generation

During the fission process there are large amounts of heat generated. Much of this heat is able to be converted into usable energy. Typically the method used to harness this thermal energy is to boil water to produce pressurized steam. The steam will then power a steam turbine that in turn will generate electricity.

Types of Reactors

Reactors are typically classified by the type of coolant that they use. In the U.S. there are currently 104 operating reactors. Of these 104, 69 are pressurized water reactors and 35 of them are boiling water reactors.

Pressurized Water Reactor (PWR)

These types of reactors are by far the most common type of Nuclear Reactors in use as of now. In these reactors ordinary water is used as both neutron moderators and coolant. The water is used as moderator and the primary coolant is separate to the water used to generate steam and to drive a turbine. In order to efficiently convert the heat produced by the Nuclear Reaction into electricity, the water that moderates the neutron and cools the fuel elements is contained at pressures 150 times greater than atmospheric pressure.

Boiling Water Reactor (BWR)

In a Boiling Water Reactor ordinary light water is used as both a moderator and coolant, like the PWR. Where it differs is that in a Boiling Water Reactor there is no separate secondary steam cycle. The water from the reactor is converted into steam and used to directly drive the generator turbine.

Nuclear Waste and Disposal

To produce the electricity in a reactor, it is necessary to split uranium atoms. This uranium used as fuel in a nuclear plant is formed into small ceramic pellets. Fission is then used to release particles of their own. These particles strike other uranium atoms and it results in splitting. During this splitting there are certain changes that take place. The particles that are left over after the atoms have split are very radioactive. Different phases and elements of the process result in different leftovers with different half lives.

Reactors that are finished with production are called spent nuclear reactors (SNF) Radioactive material in SNF falls into 3 categories, un-reacted fuel (usually uranium), fission products, activation products (notably plutonium). The fission products are the most radioactive and have the shortest half-lives. Uranium and plutonium have longer half lives but are less radioactive SNF goes from reactor to interim storage anywhere from 20–40 years. Interim storage typically consists of putting nuclear wastes into large pools of water. The water cools the radioactive isotopes and shields the environment from the radiation. After the cooling off period the high level of waste will either be reprocessed or directly disposed.

Much of the uranium and plutonium can be reprocessed and recycled as fuel to power the nuclear reactor. What cannot be salvaged will be disposed of indefinitely due to the large amounts of time that it takes for some of the waste isotopes to decay. The disposal system consists of surrounding the packaged solid waste and preventing it from moving or leaking into the environment. The packaging is typically a copper canister with a cast iron insert. The second layer consists of bentonite clay and is used as a buffer. It will protect the canister from any small movements. The last step is to place these into several hundred meters of rock. The rock stops the leaking of the material into the environment as well as to protect the canister and offer a stable environment.

Currently no country has a complete system for storing high level waste but many have plans to do so within the next 10 years.

Pros and Cons of Nuclear Power

Pros

- Phenomenal Energy Output—The energy produced from fissionable material like Uranium-235, is approximately 10 million times the energy obtained by burning same mass of coal.

- Relatively Low Operating Costs—Once built, a nuclear power plant is not an expensive energy source to fuel and operate.

- Nuclear technology is readily available—It does not have to be developed first, eliminating costs.

- Nuclear Power Generation emits very low amounts of CO_2 —The emissions of green house gases and therefore the contribution of nuclear power plants to global warming is relatively little.

- A Reliable Energy Source—Nuclear energy is a comparatively reliable energy resource, unaffected by strikes and shortages around the world, as very little is required at a time and its well distributed around the world.

- Safety—This can be looked at as a pro or a con. The results of a compromised reactor core can be catastrophic, however, the precautions and safety measures taken by the manufacturers of these facilities as well as the regulatory agencies are extremely redundant and prevent accidents very well. Statistically, nuclear power is one of the safest methods of producing energy.

Cons

- Time and Costs—The time frame needed for formalities, planning and building of a new nuclear power generation plant is very lengthy. Also, the costs associated with constructing a nuclear plant are extremely expensive.

- Nuclear Meltdowns and Disasters—A nuclear meltdown occurs when there is an acute shortage of coolant water in the nuclear reactor. This can lead to disastrous consequences, harming humans as well as the environment. The Chernobyl accident of 1986 is a constant reminder of the devastation of radiation in the event of a meltdown.

- Radioactive Waste Disposal—The safe disposal of radioactive waste is a major problem. Fission of a material like Uranium leaves by-products, which are themselves radioactive and highly harmful to the environment. Storage facilities are not sufficient to store the world's nuclear waste, which limits the amount of nuclear fuel that can be used per year.

- Preferred Terrorist Attack Target—A terrorist attack on a nuclear power plant similar to the attacks on 9/11 could have worldwide catastrophic effects. The EPR Reactor plants designed by companies such as Areva NP are intended to withstand commercial and military aircraft attacks.

- A Catalyst for Nuclear Weapons Creation—There is no guarantee that fissionable nuclear fuel supplied to a country will not fall in to the wrong hands and be used to produce weapons of mass destruction like atomic bombs and hydrogen bombs.

Nuclear Power and U.S. Energy

In 2008, the United States produced 74.23 quads of energy with nuclear energy being the 4th leading fuel to produce energy ranking after Petroleum, Dry Natural Gas, and Coal. The processes tied to nuclear energy were responsible for 8.46 quads of energy produced. The U.S. Energy consumption for 2008 was 100 quads or 1 quadrillion British Thermal Units with energy consumption as a result of the nuclear energy processes being 8.46 quads or 8.46% of the total energy consumption. This consumption level was enough to place nuclear energy as the fourth leading domestic source of energy consumed in the United States. In 2008, the United States had to import 25.99 quads of energy to close the gap between the amount of energy they produced domestically and the amount of energy that was consumed by Americans' throughout the year.

That begs the question can nuclear power be counted on to produce a larger portion of the energy consumed yearly in the United States? And if so, How long would it take to reach that level? The obvious way for Nuclear Power to see an increased importance in production of energy in the United States is to be used as a greater contributor of electricity. Since 2004, the United States has used approximately 4.0 x 109 Megawatt hours (MWh) of electricity with the United States consuming 3.95 9 MWh of electricity in 2009. Of that number, Nuclear was responsible for 7.99 x 108 MWh or 20.3% of all electricity.

Due to the present concern about greenhouse gases, the United States and countries around the world have begun looking into energy producing technologies that minimize or even eliminate carbon dioxide (CO_2)emissions. Nuclear power falls into this category since it emits a trace amount of CO_2.

Is increasing production from nuclear energy a viable candidate to help reduce the current problems with CO_2 emissions? If so, at what cost?

When discussing costs and estimates of any project there is always more than one. It is no different when discussing nuclear energy. There are estimates on the low end such as the study performed at the University of Chicago and funded by the U.S. Department of Energy and there are estimates significantly higher than that such as the estimate made by Craig Severance in his study titled "Business Risks and Costs of New Nuclear".

Factors affecting nuclear energy:

- Generating capacity

- Fuel Costs

- Increasing Fuel Costs

- CO_2 emissions tax

- Capital Costs

- Generating Capacity

Generating capacity may be the biggest hurdle as nuclear power plants operate on a daily basis at 90% of their total operating capacity meaning that any increase in energy production would have to be done through the creation of new power plants. This increase in generating capacity caused a spike in power generation equivalent to the construction of new power plants. U.S. electricity demand is projected to rise 28 percent by 2035. Maintaining nuclear energy's current 20 percent share of generation would require building about one reactor per year starting in 2016, or 20 to 25 new units by 2035.

Capacity Factor

YEAR	CAPACITY FACTOR
1980	56%
1990	66%
2000	88%
2002	>90%

Fuel Costs

The cost of Uranium is one of the main positive aspects of switching to a more invasive nuclear program. The current fuel cost associated with Uranium is less than $.005/kWh. To further enhance this aspect is the fact that an increase in the price of uranium will only have a minimal effect on the $/kWh. For Example, the doubling of the price of uranium will only increase the price/kWh from $.005 to $.0062 or an increase of 24% while doubling the cost of coal will cause the price/kWh to rise 31% and the same move in gas prices will cause an increase in price/kWh of 66%. Only if the price of Uranium rises above $100 for a prolonged period of time will the fuel cost associated to nuclear suffer.

Severance estimates the cost of fuel to be $.03/kWh. This estimate, however, includes all costs tied to the fuel from the time it is mined until the time it is disposed. The cost of enriching the uranium, disposing of the uranium and other miscellaneous costs tied to the use of uranium during the nuclear process.

Capital Costs

The study by the University of Chicago which was funded by the US Department of Energy, compared the levelized power costs of future nuclear, coal, and gas-fired power generation in the USA. Various nuclear options were cover, and for an initial ABWR or AP1000 they range from $.043/kWh to $.05/kWh on the basis of overnight capital costs of $1200 to $1500/kW, 60 year plant life, 5 year construction and 90% capacity. Coal gives $.035/kWh to $.041/kWh and gas gives $.035/kWh to $.045/kWh depending greatly on the fuel price.

The levelized cost figures include up to 29% of the overnight capital cost as interest, and the report notes that up to another 24% of the overnight capital cost needs to be added for the initial unit of a first-of-a-kind advanced design such as the AP1000 from Westinghouse.

However, the Severance study estimated capital costs for new nuclear energy to be in the neighborhood of $.17/kWh to

$.22/kWh. The increase can be seen in Severance's inclusion of decommissioning costs, property tax and waste costs.

Tax on CO2 emissions

Another potential cost savings can be found in a lower CO_2 emission per kWh. As seen in the table below a nuclear power plant emits approximately 10 times less emissions than a coal fired power plant.

The need for land is not a problem for nuclear power. Current power plants only use approximately 2 square miles. The U.S. could accomodate the current electricity demands in the U.S. and only have a footprint the size of the state of Delaware. The U.S. would need to have 512 nuclear power plants to accomplish this feat.

Conclusion

So is nuclear the answer the U.S. problem regarding CO_2 emissions? At first glance it would appear it could be difficult to determine what study of the cost of nuclear energy to believe. However, this can be decided by looking at the costs associated with many of the newest proposed plants. The reported price of six pressurized water reactors set to begin building in 2008 can shed some light on the situation. Of the six reactors, the lowest estimated capital cost was $2,444 with the highest being $5,144. It appears that Severance's numbers are closer to the current cost environment surrounding the construction of nuclear power plants. With the U.S. needing to build an additional 20 to 25 plants by 2035 just to maintain their share of an increasing United States energy consumption it does not appear likely that nuclear will be able to bite off a bigger piece of the energy consumption pie.

Companies and their Nuclear Technologies

Currently there are four nuclear reactor manufacturing companies with operations and reactor technologies in the United States. Each of these companies also offer a wide range of nuclear products and services. These companies are: GE Hitachi Nuclear Energy, Westinghouse, AREVA NP, Asea Brown Boveri/Combustion Engineering*. (ABB's nuclear power business was acquired by BNFL in 2000 and was merged into a BNFL subsidiary, Westinghouse Electric Company.) The primary technological focus of each company is their Generation III+ reactors which are relatively similar in function, but each has its own unique design and features. A generation III reactor is a development of any of the generation II nuclear reactor designs incorporating evolutionary improvements in design developed during the lifetime of the generation II reactor designs. These include improved fuel technology, superior thermal efficiency, passive safety systems and standardized design for reduced maintenance and capital costs.

Westinghouse Electric Company
Westinghouse Electric Company products and services include nuclear fuel, service and maintenance, instrumentation, controls, and advanced nuclear plant designs. The majority owner of Westinghouse is Toshiba Corporation, which purchased Westinghouse from BNFL in 2006. Westinghouse's nuclear technology is the basis for approximately half of the more than 440 operating commercial nuclear reactors worldwide. As of January 2009, in the United States, six of Westinghouse's AP1000 nuclear plants had been ordered. Also, the AP1000 had been selected as the supplier and technology of choice for a total of at least 14 new announced plants. The technology and design of the AP1000 was aimed at reducing capital costs and focused on becoming economically competitive with contemporary fossil-fueled plants. Using a passive safety system design the AP1000 requires 45% less volume to house the safety equipment. Because of its simplified design compared to a Westinghouse generation II pressurized water reactor, the AP1000 has:

- 50% fewer safety-related valves
- 35% fewer pumps
- 80% less safety related piping
- 85% less control cable
- 45% less building volume

This efficient design helps make the AP1000's footprint noticeably smaller than typical reactors. The AP1000 is projected to produce a net 1154 MWe. The AP1000's simplified design saves money and time with an accelerated construction time period of approximately 36 months, from the pouring of the concrete to the loading of the fuel.

GE Hitachi

GE Hitachi Nuclear Energy has provided advanced technology for nuclear energy for over five decades. They divide their product lines into three categories: advanced reactor technologies, nuclear services, and nuclear fuel cycle. GE Hitachi is recognized as the world's foremost developer of boiling water reactors. One such reactor is the EBSWR or Economically Simplified Boiling Water Reactor, whose design is simple yet very effective. This reactor employs Passive Safety Design features similar to those of the Westinghouse AP1000. The passively safe characteristics are mainly based on isolation condensers, which are heat exchangers that take steam from the vessel or the containment (passive containment cooling system, PCCS), condense the steam, transfer the heat to a water pool, and introduce the water into the vessel again. This means that all residual heat is transferred to the atmosphere. The ESBWR design reduces 25% of pumps, valves, and motors from previous designs and it has a referenced construction schedule of 42 months. The ESBWR uses natural circulation with no recirculation pumps or their associated piping, thereby greatly increasing design integrity and reducing overall costs. The ESBWR is currently in the U.S. design certification process unlike the AP1000 which is the only Generation III+ reactor to have received design certification in the United States. The nominal summertime output of an ESBWR is rated at 1575-1600 MWe. One single ESBWR, replacing the same amount of electricity generated through traditional sources, would reduce greenhouse emissions by an amount equivalent to taking 1.5 million cars off the road.

Areva NP

Areva is a French public multinational industrial conglomerate mainly known for nuclear power. Areva is the only company with a presence in each industrial activity linked to nuclear energy: mining, chemistry, enrichment, combustibles, services, engineering, nuclear propulsion and reactors, treatments, recycling, stabilization, and dismantling. Areva is known for their EPR or European Pressurized Reactor. The EPR has been designed to meet extremely high safety criteria. It is resistant to external hazards due to a sturdy concrete shell that can withstand commercial or military airplane impacts. The reactor building's dual-wall containment and a specific compartment isolate the core perfectly in the event of a meltdown accident. Safety is enhanced through a quadruple redundant safeguard system. The EPR reactor is a 1,650 Mwe pressurized water reactor and Areva has mastered it perfectly: they have built 87 pressurized water reactors in 11 countries of which 84 are still in operation. Areva's EPR reactor is the first Generation III+ pressurized water reactor design currently being built (four currently under construction) to answer the world's growing demand for clean and reliable electricity generation. Under construction in Finland, France and China, the EPR reactor is also being considered by the United States, United Kingdom, India and other countries for the development of their nuclear fleet. Areva announced in March 2010 the design of a new reactor type capable of breaking down actinides created as a product of nuclear fission.

Asea Brown Boveri/Combustion Engineering or ABB

ABB is the world's largest builder of electricity grids and is active in many sectors, its core businesses being in power and automation technologies. ABB is one of the largest engineering companies as well as one of the largest conglomerates in the world. Up until the sale of ABB's nuclear power business in 2000 they produced and advanced pressurized water reactor known as the System 80+. When ABB was merged into Westinghouse, the companies combined technology. Today, ABB still designs and produces qualified nuclear applications such as Electromechanical relays, Generator Circuit Breakers, and Robotic cleaners. Their generator circuit breakers such as the HEC-7C are technologically superior to all other manufacturers and have the world's highest short-circuit current capabilities. Suitable for the largest power plants, the HEC 7/8 has been developed as a system to be used in nuclear, coal fired and hydro power plants. All of these technologies are currently used in nuclear power plants and reactor stations around the world.

New projects

Most reactors on order or planned are in the Asian region, though there are major plans for new units in Europe, the USA and Russia. Significant further capacity is being created by plant upgrading. Plant life extension programs are maintaining capacity, in the US particularly. The newest plants in the U.S. are the following 5.

Watts Bar Nuclear Plant

It is TVA energy company's third nuclear power plant. Located on 1,700 acres on the northern end of Chickamauga Reservoir, in east Tennessee.The plant was named for a sandbar at Watts Island that hampered navigation on the Tennessee River until it was flooded by Watts Bar Reservoir. Groundbreaking on Watts Bar Nuclear Plant occurred in 1972, with major construction beginning a year later. Unit 1, the last commercial nuclear unit in the United States to come online in the 20th century, began commercial operation in May 1996. It iscapable of producing 1,170 megawatts of electricity, enough to serve 650,000 homes. In its 13 years of safely generating electricity, Unit 1, with an operating capacity factor of 95 percent, has produced more than 112 billion kilowatt hours of electricity. (About 8.6 billion kw hours of electricity a year. About 620 TVA employees help ensure the safe and reliable operation of Watts Bar Unit 1.

Comanche Peak unit 1 and 2

Construction of the two Westinghouse pressurized water reactors began in 1974. Unit 1, originally rated at 1,084 MWe, came online on April 17, 1990. Its current, 40-year operating license is valid until February 8, 2030. Unit 2, 1,124 MWe, followed on April 6, 1993 and is licensed to operate until February 2, 2033 when it has to renew its license. As of 2006[update] Unit 2 was the second-last power reactor to come online in the USA, followed only by Watts Bar 1.

On June 2008, the Nuclear Regulatory Comission approved a request to increase the generating capacity of units 1 and 2 by approximately 4.5% each. Unit 1 was uprated in autumn 2008 and saw a generating capacity increase from approximately 1,210 to 1,259 MWe and in Unit 2, the capacity rose from an estimated 1,208 to 1,245 MWe, was uprated in autumn 2009.

Seabrook Station Unit 1

Located on a 900-acre site in the towns of Seabrook, Hampton and Hampton Falls in New Hampshire, about 40 miles north of Boston. It began an operation in 1990. It generates about 1,094 million watts of electricity which is enough power to supply the daily needs of more than 900,000 homes

Seabrook Station opened a visitor's center called the Science & Nature Center in 1978. More than 500,000 visitors have toured the center, which offers more than 30 interactive, educational exhibits that focus on nuclear energy and the thriving ecosystem that surrounds the plant. The facility hosts an average of 2,000 to 3,000 students annually on field trips each year.

Limerick Unit

The Limerick Generating Station in Pennsylvania is located next to the Schuyckill River. The facility has two boiling water reactor units, cooled by natural draft cooling towers. When conditions are right, these cooling towers emit enough water vapor to be seen for distances of over 50 miles. The units are capable of producing almost 1,200 megawatts of power each, which combined would provide electricity to over 2 million households.

In Japan, a Troubled Nuclear Legacy

Peter Kuznick

In the following viewpoint, Peter Kuznick considers how the United States influenced Japan's relationship to nuclear technology. As the only victim of a nuclear strike, Japan is steadfastly anti-nuclear. Eisenhower's Atoms for Peace program marketed peaceful nuclear technology as a safe and practical application of this technology worldwide, while stockpiling nuclear weapons as the cornerstone of US defense policy. Japan embraced nuclear power, but the tsunami-precipitated meltdown at Fukushima has left the future of nuclear energy uncertain for the Japanese. Kuznick is associate professor of history at American University, director of the Nuclear Studies Institute, founder of the Committee for a National Discussion of Nuclear History and Current Policy, and cofounder of the Nuclear Education Project.

As you read, consider the following questions:

1. Why did the United States offer to build a nuclear power plant for Japan? What was the larger context?
2. Did Japan embrace this idea immediately? How did the United States "sell" nuclear power to Japan?
3. Why does the author call Fukushima a "reckoning"?

"Japan's nuclear history in perspective: Eisenhower and atoms for war and peace," by Peter Kuznick, Bulletin of the Atomic Scientists, April 13, 2011. Reprinted by permission.

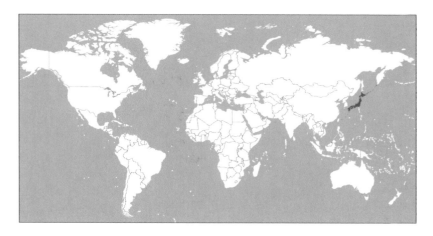

I t is tragic that Japan, the most fiercely antinuclear country on the planet, with its Peace Constitution, three non-nuclear principles, and commitment to nuclear disarmament, is being hit with the most dangerous and prolonged nuclear crisis in the past quarter-century—one whose damage might still exceed that of Chernobyl 25 years ago. But Japan's antinuclearism has always rested upon a Faustian bargain, marked by dependence on the United States, which has been the most unabashedly pro-nuclear country on the planet for the past 66 years. It is in the strange relationship between these two oddly matched allies that the roots and meaning of the Fukushima crisis lay buried.

Japan embarked on its nuclear energy program during the presidency of Dwight Eisenhower, a man now best remembered, ironically, for warning about the rise of the very military-industrial complex he did so much to create. Eisenhower is also the only US president to have criticized the atomic bombing of Hiroshima and Nagasaki. Fearing the bombings would destroy the prospects for friendly post-war relations with Russia, at one point he advocated international control of atomic energy and turning the existing US stockpile over to the United Nations for destruction.

Yet by the time he took office in 1953, Eisenhower's views on nuclear weapons had changed. Not wanting to see the United

States "choke itself to death piling up military expenditures" and assuming that any war with the Soviet Union would quickly turn nuclear, he shifted emphasis from costly conventional military capabilities to massive nuclear retaliation by a fortified Strategic Air Command. Whereas President Harry Truman had considered nuclear arms to be weapons of last resort, Eisenhower's "New Look" made them the foundation of US defense strategy.

Just like a bullet?

On occasion, Eisenhower spoke almost cavalierly about using nuclear weapons. In 1955, he told a reporter: "Yes of course they would be used. In any combat where these things can be used on strictly military targets and for strictly military purposes, I see no reason why they shouldn't be used just exactly as you would use a bullet or anything else." When Eisenhower suggested to Winston Churchill's emissary Jock Colville that "there was no distinction between 'conventional' weapons and atomic weapons: all weapons in due course become conventional," Colville recalled, horrified, "I could hardly believe my ears."

Eisenhower began transferring control of the atomic stockpile from the Atomic Energy Commission (AEC) to the military. Europeans were terrified that the United States would start a nuclear war, which Eisenhower threatened to do over Korea, over the Suez Canal, and twice over the Taiwan Strait islands of Quemoy and Matsu. European allies begged Eisenhower to show restraint.

Public revulsion at the normalization of nuclear war threatened to derail the Eisenhower administration's plans. The minutes of a March 1953 meeting of the National Security Council (NSC) stated: "the President and Secretary [John Foster] Dulles were in complete agreement that somehow or other the tabu [sic] which surrounds the use of atomic weapons would have to be destroyed. While Secretary Dulles admitted that in the present state of world opinion we could not use an A-bomb, we should make every effort now to dissipate this feeling."

Atoms for Peace buried in radioactive ash

Eisenhower decided that the best way to destroy that taboo was to shift the focus from military uses of nuclear energy to socially beneficial applications. Stefan Possony, Defense Department consultant to the Psychological Strategy Board, had argued: "the atomic bomb will be accepted far more readily if at the same time atomic energy is being used for constructive ends." On December 8, 1953, Eisenhower delivered his "Atoms for Peace" speech at the United Nations. He promised that the United States would devote "its entire heart and mind to find the way by which the miraculous inventiveness of man shall not be dedicated to his death, but consecrated to his life." He pledged to spread the benefits of peaceful atomic power at home and abroad.

But the subsequent March 1954 Bravo test almost derailed those plans. Fallout from the US hydrogen-bomb test contaminated 236 Marshall Islanders and 23 Japanese fisherman aboard the Daigo Fukuryu Maru ("Lucky Dragon no. 5"), which was 85 miles away from the detonation and outside the designated danger zone. A panic ensued when irradiated tuna was sold in Japanese cities and eaten by scores of people.

The international community was appalled by the bomb test. Belgian diplomat Paul-Henri Spaak warned, "If something is not done to revive the idea of the President's speech—the idea that America wants to use atomic energy for peaceful purposes— America is going to be synonymous in Europe with barbarism and horror." Indian Prime Minister Jawaharlal Nehru declared that US leaders were "dangerous self-centered lunatics" who would "blow up any people or country who came in the way of their policy."

Eisenhower told the NSC in May 1954, "Everybody seems to think that we are skunks, saber-rattlers, and warmongers." Dulles complained, "Comparisons are now being made between ours and Hitler's military machine."

Criticism was fiercest in Japan. In Tokyo's Suginami ward, housewives began circulating petitions to ban hydrogen bombs.

The movement caught on across the country. By the next year, an astounding 32 million people, or one-third of Japan's population, had signed petitions against hydrogen bombs.

Long-suppressed rage over the 1945 atomic bombings, squelched by US occupation authorities' total ban on discussion of the bombings, had finally erupted. The Operations Coordinating Board of the NSC recommended that the United States contain the damage by waging a "vigorous offensive on the non-war uses of atomic energy" and even offer to build Japan an experimental nuclear reactor. AEC Commissioner Thomas Murray concurred, proclaiming, "Now, while the memory of Hiroshima and Nagasaki remain so vivid, construction of such a power plant in a country like Japan would be a dramatic and Christian gesture which could lift all of us far above the recollection of the carnage of those cities."

Selling the peaceful atom in Japan

The *Washington Post* applauded Murray's idea as a way to "divert the mind of man from his present obsession with the armaments race." "Many Americans are now aware ... that the dropping of the atomic bombs on Japan was not necessary. ... How better to make a contribution to amends than by offering Japan the means for the peaceful utilization of atomic energy. How better, indeed, to dispel the impression in Asia that the United States regards Orientals merely as nuclear cannon fodder!"

Murray and Rep. Sidney Yates (Democrat of Illinois) suggested locating the first electricity-producing nuclear power plant in Hiroshima. In early 1955, Yates introduced legislation to build a 60,000-kilowatt generating plant there that would "make the atom an instrument for kilowatts rather than killing." By June, the United States and Japan had signed an agreement to work together on research and development of atomic energy.

But selling this idea to the Japanese people would not be so easy. When the US Embassy, US Information Service (USIS), and CIA launched their vigorous campaign to promote nuclear energy in Japan, they turned to Matsutaro Shoriki, the father of Japanese baseball, who ran the *Yomiuri Shimbun* newspaper and the Nippon Television Network. After two years' imprisonment as a Class-A war criminal, Shoriki had been released without trial; his virulent anti-communism helped redeem him in American eyes (see Tetsuo Arima, "Shoriki's Campaign to Promote Nuclear Power in Japan and CIA Psychological Warfare," unpublished paper presented at Tokyo University of Economics, November 25, 2006). Shoriki's newspaper agreed to co-sponsor the much-hyped US exhibit welcoming the atom back to Japan on November 1, 1955 with a Shinto purification ceremony in Tokyo. The US ambassador read a message from Eisenhower declaring the exhibit "a symbol of our countries' mutual determination that the great power of the atom shall henceforward be dedicated to the arts of peace."

After six weeks in Tokyo, the exhibit traveled to Hiroshima and six other cities. It highlighted the peaceful applications of nuclear energy for generating electricity, treating cancer, preserving food, controlling insects, and advancing scientific research. Military applications were scrupulously avoided. The nuclear future looked safe, abundant, exciting, and peaceful. The turnout exceeded expectations. In Kyoto, the USIS reported, 155,000 people braved snow and rain to attend.

The steady spate of films, lectures, and articles proved enormously successful.

Officials reported, "The change in opinion on atomic energy from 1954 to 1955 was spectacular … atom hysteria was almost eliminated and by the beginning of 1956, Japanese opinion was brought to popular acceptance of the peaceful uses of atomic energy."

Such exultation proved premature. Antinuclear organizing by left-wing political parties and trade unions resonated with the public. An April 1956 USIS survey found that 60 percent of Japanese believed nuclear energy would prove "more of a curse than a boon to mankind" and only 25 percent thought the United States was "making sincere efforts" at nuclear disarmament. The

Mainichi newspaper blasted the campaign: "First, baptism with radioactive rain, then a surge of shrewd commercialism in the guise of 'atoms for peace' from abroad." The newspaper called on the Japanese people to "calmly scrutinize what is behind the atomic energy race now being staged by the 'white hands' in Japan."

But intensified USIS activities over the coming years began to bear fruit. A classified report on the US propaganda campaign showed that in 1956, 70 percent of Japanese equated "atom" with "harmful," but by 1958, the number had dropped to 30 percent. Wanting their country to be a modern scientific-industrial power and knowing Japan lacked energy resources, the public allowed itself to be convinced that nuclear power was safe and clean. It had forgotten the lessons of Hiroshima and Nagasaki.

In 1954, the Japanese government began funding a nuclear research program. In December 1955, it passed the Atomic Energy Basic Law, establishing the Japan Atomic Energy Commission (JAEC). Shoriki became minister of state for atomic energy and first chair of the JAEC. Japan purchased its first commercial reactor from Britain but quickly switched to US-designed light water reactors. By mid-1957, the government had contracted to buy 20 additional reactors.

In the United States, the AEC aggressively marketed nuclear power as a magic elixir that would power vehicles, feed the hungry, light the cities, heal the sick, and excavate the planet. Eisenhower unveiled plans for an atomic-powered merchant ship and an atomic airplane. In July 1955, the United States generated its first commercial nuclear power. In October 1956, Eisenhower informed the United Nations that the United States had agreements with 37 nations to build atomic reactors and was negotiating with 14 more.

By 1958, the United States was becoming almost giddy with the prospect of planetary excavation under the AEC's Project Plowshare, which proposed to use peaceful nuclear blasts to build harbors, free inaccessible oil deposits, create huge underground reservoirs, and construct a bigger and better Panama Canal. Some wanted to alter weather patterns by exploding a 20-megaton bomb alongside the eye of a hurricane. One Weather Bureau scientist proposed a plan to accelerate melting of the polar icecaps by detonating 10-megaton bombs. Only Eisenhower's reluctance to unilaterally break a Soviet-initiated nuclear test moratorium halted this sheer folly.

Still, Project Plowshare achieved its goals. Lewis Strauss, chairman of the AEC, admitted that Plowshare was intended to "highlight the peaceful applications of nuclear explosive devices and thereby create a climate of world opinion that is more favorable to weapons development and tests."

Atoms for Peace masks nuclear weapons buildup

Under the cover of the peaceful atom, Eisenhower pursued the most rapid and reckless nuclear escalation in history. The US arsenal went from a little more than 1,000 nuclear weapons when he took office to approximately 22,000 when he left. But even that figure is misleading. Procurements authorized by Eisenhower continued into the 1960s, making him responsible for the levels reached during the Kennedy administration—more than 30,000 nuclear weapons. In terms of pure megatonnage, the United States amassed the equivalent of 1,360,000 Hiroshima bombs in 1961.

Few know that Eisenhower had delegated to theater commanders and other specified commanders the authority to launch a nuclear attack if they believed it mandated by circumstances and were out of communication with the president or if the president had been incapacitated. With Eisenhower's approval, some of these theater commanders had in turn delegated similar authority to lower commanders (I am grateful to Dan Ellsberg for this information). And given the fact that there were then no locks on nuclear weapons, many more people had the actual power, if not the authority, to launch a nuclear attack, including pilots, squadron leaders, base commanders, and carrier commanders.

In 1960, Eisenhower approved the first Single Integrated Operational Plan, which stipulated deploying US strategic nuclear forces in a simultaneous strike against the Sino-Soviet bloc within the first 24 hours of a war. The Joint Chiefs were subsequently asked to estimate the death toll from such an attack. The numbers were shocking: 325 million dead in the Soviet Union and China, another 100 million in Eastern Europe, 100 million from fallout in Western Europe, and up to another 100 million from fallout in countries bordering the Soviet Union—more than 600 million in total.

The price of denial

While Americans were preparing for nuclear annihilation, the Japanese were living in their own form of denial. From its shaky beginnings in the 1950s, the Japanese nuclear power industry flourished in the 1960s and 1970s and continued to grow thereafter. Prior to the tsunami-precipitated Fukushima accident last month, Japan had 54 functioning nuclear power reactors that generated 30 percent of its electricity; some projected it would not be long before Japan reached 50 percent. But the terrible nuclear catastrophe in Fukushima has forced the Japanese to deal for a third time with the nightmarish side of the nuclear age and the fact that their nuclear program was born not only in the fantasy of clean, safe power, but also in the willful forgetting of Hiroshima and Nagasaki and the buildup of the US nuclear arsenal.

A reckoning with Japan's nuclear legacy is now taking place. Hopefully, the Japanese will move forward from this tragedy to set a path toward both green energy and repudiation of deterrence under the US nuclear umbrella, much as they blazed a path with their Peace Constitution and antinuclearism following the horrors of World War II.

Flaws in the Nuclear Non-Proliferation Treaty (NPT)

Linda Gunter

In the following viewpoint, Linda Gunther points out a glaring flaw compromising the Treaty on the Non-Proliferation of Nuclear Weapons (NPT). According to Article IV, nations that promise not to develop nuclear weapons have an inalienable right to pursue peaceful nuclear technology. The problem is that nuclear energy has served as a back door to weapons production. For example, India, a country that did not sign, has weapons and is still allowed to participate in the nuclear market. Iran has signed but cannot. This inconsistency is a major flaw in the treaty. Gunter is an environmental leader who founded the international advocacy nonprofit Beyond Nuclear in 2007. She is published regularly on AlterNet, the Daily Kos, and OpEdNews.

As you read, consider the following questions:

1. What is Article IV of the Treaty on the Non-Proliferation of Nuclear Weapons designed to accomplish?
2. Why is Article IV flawed and prone to loopholes and inconsistencies?
3. Are there any other problems with the treaty's enforcement, according to this article?

This week, the nuclear Non-Proliferation Treaty (NPT) will undergo a review that has taken place every five years since the treaty went into effect in 1970. Delegates from around the world will gather from May 3-28 at the United Nations in New York to assess the status of the treaty. The nuclear activities of Iran, a signatory to the treaty, are expected to play a major role in the discussions with Iran's president, Mahmoud Ahmadinejad, expected to participate and speak early in the conference.

What likely will not happen is a revision of the treaty's Article IV, which states: "Nothing in this Treaty shall be interpreted as affecting the inalienable right of all the Parties to the Treaty to develop research, production and use of nuclear energy for peaceful purposes. . ."

In effect, Article IV offers a nuclear reward to non-nuclear weapons countries who sign the treaty; promise never to make the bomb and you can build and operate nuclear reactors. Since the materials, and to a certain degree, the processing involved in arriving at fuel for a civilian reactor or to create an atomic bomb are basically the same, a civilian program can lead to—and has led to—the covert development of nuclear weapons. Examples of this pathway include India, Pakistan, Israel and North Korea—none of whom are signatories to the NPT. (South Africa also developed nuclear weapons from its civilian nuclear program but has since dismantled its arsenal and is now a NPT signatory.

Some, including Sergio Duarte, the U.N. high commissioner for non-proliferation, argue that Article IV is the cornerstone of the NPT on which the success of the entire treaty depends. But Dominque Lalanne, Director of Research in nuclear and particle physics at the French Center for Scientific Research, contends that Article IV is in fact the problem, because, Lalanne says, "nuclear power is the way to nuclear weapons".

Today, the conundrum of Article IV is epitomized by two countries—India and Iran—and their differing and controversial approach to the development of "peaceful nuclear energy."

Nuclear Power in the United States

In the post-World War II era, the Atomic Energy Commission was created to explore peaceful opportunities for the same nuclear materials the U.S. used in Japan at the end of the war. Now almost 70 years later, there are 104 nuclear reactors harnessing that same power of atomic fission to meet nearly one-fifth of the U.S.'s commercial energy needs.

The U.S. Navy led the way with ventures in nuclear electricity generation soon after the war. The year 1957 would see the country's first commercial generation of nuclear power at the Shippingport Atomic Power Station as part of President Dwight Eisenhower's Atoms for Peace program. Operating on the Ohio River under the Duquesne Light Company, Shippingport reliably supplied nuclear energy to the Pittsburgh area for 25 years before being retired in 1982.

Shippingport broadened opportunities for atomic research and paved the way for new nuclear plant construction. Forty-six nuclear reactors were commissioned around the country in the 1980s alone. By the time of Shippingport's decommissioning in 1989, 109 nuclear reactors were generating about 19 percent of the nation's electricity, becoming the second-largest power source in the U.S., with coal still the frontrunner.

The construction of new nuclear plants slowed drastically after the 1980s, as demand for new units fell and nuclear opposition grew around the country. The events at Three Mile Island (Pennsylvania) and Chernobyl (Ukraine) in 1979 and 1986, respectively, raised concerns about the safety of nuclear power and fueled anti-nuclear dissenters.

The U.S. nuclear industry has since proved that nuclear energy is a safe and reliable power source. One hundred and four nuclear reactors currently operate in 31 states, generating about 19 percent of electricity in the U.S., including more than 70 percent of the nation's carbon-free electricity. The total U.S. nuclear production amounts to more than 800 billion kilowatt-hours as the third-largest electrical energy source behind coal and gas.

"A Brief History of Nuclear Power in the U.S.," Duke Energy Corporation, July 31, 2012.

In 2005, the then Bush administration initiated an agreement with India in apparent defiance of the terms of the NPT to which India is not a signatory.

Explains the Council on Foreign Relations:

The U.S. Congress on October 1, 2008, gave final approval to an agreement facilitating nuclear cooperation between the United States and India. The deal is seen as a watershed in U.S.-India relations and introduces a new aspect to international nonproliferation efforts. First introduced in the joint statement released by President Bush and Indian Prime Minister Manmohan Singh on July 18, 2005, the deal lifts a three-decade U.S. moratorium on nuclear trade with India. It provides U.S. assistance to India's civilian nuclear energy program, and expands U.S.-India cooperation in energy and satellite technology.

As a result, India is being actively solicited as a client by Russia, France and the United States all of which are signatories to the NPT. Although not a signatory, India is recognized as a nuclear weapons state in possession of at least 50 missiles and maybe more. Thus, the "inalienable right" is available not only to NPT signatories that renounce nuclear weapons, but also to non-signatories who don't.

Iran, by contrast, is an NPT signatory that claims to be exercising its "inalienable right" to develop nuclear energy. However, much of the world suspects that Iran is using this right as a cover to make nuclear weapons. Negotiations with Iran have see-sawed over the past several years while intelligence experts continue to predict when, rather than if, Iran will have the bomb.

Pakistan may also now be considered part of this small, contentious group. On the very eve of the NPT review conference, China announced it would build two reactors in Pakistan, redressing the "balance" upset by the U.S.-India deal. This move further exemplifies the inevitable arms race that springs from the development of civilian nuclear energy.

The NPT may be further compromised by the official nuclear weapons states themselves that are party to the treaty—the U.S., Russia, China, France and the United Kingdom—who in some cases, and despite a treaty-bound obligation to disarm, continue to fund and even to reinforce their nuclear weapons sectors. France is backing the development of the new M51 missile that has a greater range than its predecessors. The Obama administration has requested a spending increase of $7 billion for, among other projects, a new plutonium production facility in Los Alamos, New Mexico. (However, the recent announcement of Obama's Nuclear Posture Review stated definitively that the U.S. would not expand its nuclear weapons arsenal).

Further undermining the effectiveness of Article IV is that the United Nations tends to act as a kindly landlord, allowing any signatory to leave the NPT fold provided it gives three months' notice. Thus North Korea, which signed the treaty as a non-weapons state in 1985, chose to exit the treaty in 2003 once it had developed the bomb. As with Iran, protracted back-and-forth negotiations with North Korea have resulted largely in exasperation but no meaningful progress and much nuclear saber-rattling by the North Korean government.

This April, President Obama invited leaders from 47 countries to a global Nuclear Security Summit in Washington. The primary subject under discussion was nuclear terrorism—the perpetual threat of terrorists laying their hands on and using nuclear materials either in an actual nuclear weapon or in what is known as a "dirty bomb" (a conventional explosive device containing radioactive materials). There was general agreement that the danger was real and all 47 countries agreed to make serious—but voluntary—efforts to secure nuclear materials from terrorists within the next four years.

The problem of nuclear terrorism is a very real, alarming and urgent one. A typical 1,000 megawatt nuclear reactor produces at least 40 bombs-worth of plutonium a year, according to calculations done by Tom Cochran, the director of the Natural Resources Defense Council's nuclear program. Poorly guarded nuclear materials in the former Soviet Union are suspected already to have fallen into the hands of known terrorist groups.

The notorious "A. Q. Khan Network," allegedly masterminded by the eponymous Pakistani nuclear physicist, may have led to the illegal transfer of unknown quantities of nuclear materials onto the global black market.

The question remains just how these dangerous nuclear materials can be secured simultaneously with the marketing and expansion of civilian nuclear technology to countries both inside and outside of the NPT family of signatories. This contradiction is at the heart of the flaw in Article IV.

Disparity Between Nuclear and Non-nuclear Nations Impedes NPT

Lawrence Wittner

In the following viewpoint, Lawrence Wittner traces the context and aims of the Nuclear Non-Proliferation Treaty (NPT). By the mid 1960s, many nations either had a nuclear weapon or were on a path to developing one. As the two leading post-war nuclear powers, the United States and the former Soviet Union both sensed the potential dangers of nuclear proliferation. Wishing to preserve joint monopoly on nuclear weapons, the two superpowers found common ground on the NPT. Non-nuclear nations argue this created a double standard, wherein nuclear nations keep their weapons while forbidding others to do develop them. Thus, disarmament became an important part of the revised NPT. Wittner is professor of history emeritus at SUNY Albany.

As you read, consider the following questions:

1. Why did theUnited States and former Soviet Union agree on the need to contain nuclear weapons?
2. Did the NPT work? How many nations have gained nuclear weapons since it was ratified?
3. Why did some nations feel the NPT was unfair?

The opening this May of the nuclear Non-Proliferation Treaty (NPT) review conference at the United Nations seems likely to

"The Nuclear Non-Proliferation Treaty, Past and Present," by Lawrence Wittner, TheHuffingtonPost.com, Inc, May 25, 2011. Reprinted by permission.

feature a conflict that has simmered for decades between nuclear nations and non-nuclear nations.

By the mid-1960s, five nations had developed a nuclear weapons capability: the United States, the Soviet Union, Britain, France, and, most recently, China. But numerous other nations were giving serious consideration to joining the nuclear club. They included Argentina, Brazil, Egypt, India, Israel, Pakistan, South Africa, and West Germany. Millions of people and many governments feared that the nuclear arms race—already dangerous enough—was on the verge of spiraling totally out of control.

In this context, the U.S. and Soviet governments suddenly found something they could agree upon. Having amassed vast nuclear arsenals for their Cold War confrontation with one another, both decided that it would be a good idea if other nations refrained from developing nuclear weapons. Thus, in the fall of 1965, the two governments submitted nonproliferation treaties to the U.N. General Assembly. "Both superpowers really got behind the Nonproliferation Treaty," recalled U.S. Secretary of State Dean Rusk, "because we and the Soviets basically were on the same wavelength."

But the non-nuclear powers sharply objected to the U.S. and Soviet proposals, which they pointed out, correctly, would establish a two-tier system. Alva Myrdal, Sweden's disarmament minister and a leading proponent of nuclear disarmament, declared that "the non-aligned nations . . . strongly believe that disarmament measures should be a matter of mutual renunciation." They did not want a treaty that "would leave the present five nuclear-weapon parties free to continue to build up their arsenals." The governments of numerous NATO nations raised the same objection. Willy Brandt, West Germany's foreign minister, maintained that a nonproliferation treaty was justified "only if the nuclear states regard it as a step toward restrictions of their own armaments and toward disarmament." In short, non-nuclear nations were unwilling to forgo the nuclear option in the absence of a similar commitment by the nuclear nations.

As a result, the NPT was reshaped to provide for mutual obligations on the part of non-nuclear and nuclear nations. Under its terms, each non-nuclear signatory pledged "not to make or acquire nuclear weapons," as well as to accept a safeguard system, administered by the International Atomic Energy Agency, to prevent diversion of nuclear material from nuclear reactors to nuclear weapons development. Furthermore, Article VI of the final version provided that nuclear signatories would "pursue negotiations in good faith at an early date on effective measures regarding cessation of the nuclear arms race and disarmament."

On June 12, 1968, this revised NPT, now incorporating provisions for both nonproliferation and disarmament, swept through the U.N. General Assembly by a vote of 95 to 4, with 21 abstentions. Although, ominously, a number of nations with nuclear ambitions refused to ratify the treaty, the NPT did provide an important milestone in global efforts to avert nuclear catastrophe.

In some ways, the NPT was a success. After it went into force in 1970, almost all nations capable of building nuclear weapons rejected this option. Furthermore, through disarmament treaties and individual action, the nuclear nations divested themselves of a significant number of their nuclear weapons.

Even so, thanks to a lingering belief that national security ultimately lies in military strength, nations have resisted honoring their full obligations under the NPT. The nuclear powers delayed implementing their rhetorical commitment to full-scale nuclear disarmament. Meanwhile, some non-nuclear nations, charging the nuclear powers with hypocrisy, began to develop nuclear weapons themselves. Today, 42 years after the signing of the NPT, more than 23,000 nuclear weapons remain in existence and the number of nuclear powers has grown from five to nine.

Thus, the NPT review conference this May could simply continue the old game of duplicity and delay. Nuclear nations could avoid making plans to eliminate their very substantial nuclear arsenals, while demanding that other countries remain non-nuclear. Non-nuclear nations could point to the failure of the nuclear nations to disarm and use that as their justification for joining the nuclear club.

But there is an alternative. The world public might decide that enough is enough—that it's time to move beyond the cautious, half-way measures of the past and bring an end to the terrible danger of nuclear annihilation. That would require a massive outpouring of public sentiment, this May and in the following months, demanding nothing less than the abolition of nuclear weapons. Already there are signs that such an outpouring has begun, with gatherings of disarmament activists from around the world meeting in New York City this coming Friday and Saturday, and a large nuclear disarmament rally and march, from Times Square to the United Nations, occurring on Sunday, May 2. These and other expressions of antinuclear sentiment would provide a solid basis on which reluctant government officials might finally do what they should long ago have done: take effective action to build a nuclear weapons-free world.

The Comprehensive Nuclear Test Ban Treaty: Then and Now

Mary Beth Nikitin

In the following excerpted viewpoint, Mary Beth Nikitin provides a detailed historical overview of nuclear test treaties. She explains that bans on testing nuclear weapons is "the oldest item on the nuclear arms control agenda." Although earlier versions of such treaties have gone into effect, the latest iteration called the Comprehensive Nuclear Test Ban Treaty (CTBT) has stalled somewhat. This treaty would ban any detonation of a nuclear device. After the fall of the Soviet Union, president Clinton backed this treaty, but the Senate rejected it. Currently, 183 nations back the treaty, but it lacks the support of all 44 states that would need to ratify it. North Korea's recent activities have been in flagrant violation of the treaty, raising doubts that nations with nuclear ambitions will sign on. Nikitin is an analyst in WMD Nonproliferation in the Foreign Affairs, Defense and Trade Division of the Congressional Research Service (CRS), Library of Congress. She writes on nuclear nonproliferation topics including the nuclear fuel cycle, nuclear cooperation agreements, nuclear security, and North Korea nuclear issues.

"Comprehensive Nuclear-Test-Ban Treaty: Background and Current Developments," by Mary Beth D. Nikitin, Congressional Research Service, September 1, 2016. Reprinted by permission.

As you read, consider the following questions:

1. What treaties preceded the CTBT, and how were they different?
2. What are some pros and cons of the CTBT?
3. How does the author think the treaty will affect nuclear nonproliferation and disarmament?

Summary

A ban on all nuclear tests is the oldest item on the nuclear arms control agenda. Three treaties that entered into force between 1963 and 1990 limit, but do not ban, such tests. In 1996, the United Nations General Assembly adopted the Comprehensive Nuclear-Test-Ban Treaty (CTBT), which would ban all nuclear explosions. In 1997, President Clinton sent the CTBT to the Senate, which rejected it in October 1999. In a speech in Prague in April 2009, President Obama said, "My administration will immediately and aggressively pursue U.S. ratification of the Comprehensive Test Ban Treaty." However, while the Administration has indicated it wants to begin a CTBT "education" campaign with a goal of securing Senate advice and consent to ratification, it has not pressed for a vote on the treaty and there were no hearings on it in the 111th, 112th, or 113th Congresses. There will be at least one hearing in the 114th Congress—a Senate Foreign Relations Committee hearing on the CTBT planned for September 7, 2016.

As of August 2016, 183 states had signed the CTBT and 164, including Russia, had ratified it. However, entry into force requires ratification by 44 states specified in the treaty, of which 41 had signed the treaty and 36 had ratified. India, North Korea, and Pakistan have not signed the treaty. Nine conferences have been held to facilitate entry into force, every other year, most recently on September 29, 2015. In years between these conferences, some foreign ministers meet to promote entry into force of the CTBT. A ministerial meeting was held on June 13, 2016, to commemorate the 20th anniversary of the signing of the CTBT.

Nuclear testing has a long history, beginning in 1945. The Natural Resources Defense Council states that the United States conducted 1,030 nuclear tests, the Soviet Union 715, the United Kingdom 45, France 210, and China 45. (Of the U.K. tests, 24 were held jointly with the United States and are not included in the foregoing U.S. total.) Congress passed and President George H.W. Bush signed legislation in 1992 that established a unilateral moratorium on U.S. nuclear testing. Russia claims it has not tested since 1990. In 1998, India and Pakistan announced several nuclear tests. Each declared a test moratorium; neither has signed the CTBT. North Korea announced that it conducted nuclear tests in 2006, 2009, 2013, and 2016. Since 1997, the United States has held 28 "subcritical experiments" at the Nevada National Security Site, most recently in August 2014, to study how plutonium behaves under pressures generated by explosives. It asserts these experiments do not violate the CTBT because they cannot produce a self-sustaining chain reaction. Russia reportedly held some such experiments since 1998.

The Stockpile Stewardship Program seeks to maintain confidence in the safety, security, and reliability of U.S. nuclear weapons without nuclear testing. Its budget is listed as "Weapons Activities" within the request of the National Nuclear Security Administration, a semiautonomous component of the Department of Energy. Congress addresses nuclear weapon issues in the annual National Defense Authorization Act and the Energy and Water Development Appropriations Act. The FY2017 request for Weapons Activities was $9.243 billion; on a comparable basis, the FY2016-enacted amount was $8.846 billion. Congress also considers a U.S. contribution to a global system to monitor possible nuclear tests, operated by the Preparatory Commission for the Comprehensive Nuclear-Test-Ban Treaty Organization. The FY2016 request for the contribution was $33.0 million.

This report will be updated occasionally. This update reflects the FY2017 budget request and developments through August 2016. CRS Report RL34394, Comprehensive Nuclear-Test-Ban Treaty:

Issues and Arguments, by Jonathan E. Medalia, presents pros and cons in detail. CRS Report R40612, Comprehensive Nuclear-Test-Ban Treaty: Updated "Safeguards" and Net Assessments, by Jonathan E. Medalia, discusses safeguards—unilateral steps to maintain U.S. nuclear security consistent with nuclear testing treaties—and their relationship to the CTBT. CRS Report R43948, Energy and Water Development: FY2016 Appropriations for Nuclear Weapons Stockpile Stewardship, by Jonathan E. Medalia, and CRS Report R44442, Energy and Water Development: FY2017 Appropriations for Nuclear Weapons Activities, by Amy F. Woolf, provide details on stockpile stewardship.

[…]

Most Recent Developments

The Comprehensive Nuclear-Test-Ban Treaty Organization (CTBTO) PrepCom's international monitoring system detected data indicating that North Korea had conducted a nuclear test on January 6, 2016. The CTBTO PrepCom held a symposium for experts called Science and Diplomacy for Peace and Security in January 2016.[1] The spring CTBTO PrepCom meeting was a "20 Year Ministerial" from June 13-14, 2016, to mark the 20th anniversary of the opening for signature of the Comprehensive Nuclear-Test-Ban Treaty (CTBT) and to explore options for advancing its entry into force.[2] At that meeting, Pakistan reiterated its stance that "it will not be the first in its region to resume nuclear testing." On August 29, 2016, the CTBTO PrepCom held an international conference—On the International Day Against Nuclear Testing—in Almaty, Kazakhstan, to mark 25 years after the nuclear test site in Kazakhstan was closed down. The United States is working with other countries to draft a UN Security Council Resolution marking the 20th year after the signing of the CTBT on September 24. The CTBTO PrepCom will meet in November 2016.

[…]

History

While the CTBT was opened for signature in 1996,[3] it has not entered into force, leaving a ban on nuclear testing as the oldest item on the arms control agenda. Efforts to curtail tests have been made since the 1940s. In the 1950s, the United States and Soviet Union conducted hundreds of hydrogen bomb tests. The radioactive fallout from these tests spurred worldwide protest. These pressures, plus a desire to improve U.S.-Soviet relations in the wake of the Cuban Missile Crisis of 1962, led to the Limited Test Ban Treaty of 1963, which banned nuclear explosions in the atmosphere, in space, and under water. The Threshold Test Ban Treaty, signed in 1974, banned underground nuclear weapons tests having an explosive force of more than 150 kilotons, the equivalent of 150,000 tons of TNT, 10 times the force of the Hiroshima bomb. The Peaceful Nuclear Explosions Treaty, signed in 1976, extended the 150-kiloton limit to nuclear explosions for peaceful purposes. President Carter did not pursue ratification of these treaties, preferring to negotiate a comprehensive test ban treaty, or CTBT, a ban on all nuclear explosions. When agreement on a CTBT seemed near, however, he pulled back, bowing to arguments that continued testing was needed to maintain reliability of existing weapons, to develop new weapons, and for other purposes. President Reagan raised concerns about U.S. ability to monitor the two unratified treaties and late in his term started negotiations on new verification protocols. These two treaties were ratified in 1990.

With the end of the Cold War, the need for improved warheads dropped and pressures for a CTBT grew. The U.S.S.R. and France began nuclear test moratoria in October 1990 and April 1992, respectively. In early 1992, many in Congress favored a one-year test moratorium. The effort led to the Hatfield-Exon-Mitchell amendment to the FY1993 Energy and Water Development Appropriations Bill, which banned testing before July 1, 1993, set conditions on a resumption of testing, banned testing after September 1996 unless another nation tested, and required the President to report to Congress annually on a plan to achieve a

CTBT by September 30, 1996. President George H. W. Bush signed the bill into law (P.L. 102-377) October 2, 1992. The CTBT was negotiated in the Conference on Disarmament. It was adopted by the U.N. General Assembly on September 10, 1996, and was opened for signature on September 24, 1996. As of August 2016, 183 states had signed it and 164 had ratified.[4]

[…]

CTBT Pros and Cons

The CTBT is contentious. For a detailed analysis of the case for and against the treaty, see CRS Report RL34394, Comprehensive Nuclear-Test-Ban Treaty: Issues and Arguments, by Jonathan E. Medalia. Key arguments include the following:

Can the United States maintain deterrence without testing? The treaty's supporters hold that the U.S. stockpile stewardship program can maintain existing, tested weapons without further testing. Indeed, as noted above, as of August 2015 the weapons laboratories had completed 19 annual assessments of the stockpile, with the 20th in progress. Treaty supporters claim that these weapons meet any deterrent needs, so that new types are not needed. Opponents maintain that there can be no confidence in existing warheads because many minor modifications over time will change them from tested versions. As a result, some opponents argue that testing is needed to restore and maintain confidence, while others believe that testing may become needed and the option to return to testing must not be ruled out. Opponents see deterrence as dynamic, requiring new types of nuclear weapons to counter new threats, and assert that these weapons must be tested.

Are monitoring and verification capability sufficient? "Monitoring" refers to technical capability; "verification" to its adequacy to maintain security. Supporters hold that advances in monitoring, such as the rollout of the International Monitoring System, make it hard for an evader to conduct undetected tests. They claim that any such tests would be too small to affect the strategic balance. Opponents see many opportunities for evasion, such as detonating an explosion in a large underground cavity to muffle its seismic waves. They believe that clandestine tests of even small weapons could put the United States at a serious disadvantage.

How might the treaty affect nuclear nonproliferation and disarmament? Supporters claim that the treaty makes technical contributions to nonproliferation, such as limiting weapons programs; some supporters believe that nonproliferation requires progress toward nuclear disarmament, with the treaty a key step. They note that all NATO members excepting the United States have ratified the CTBT. Opponents believe that a strong nuclear deterrent is essential for nonproliferation because it reduces the incentive for friends and foes alike to build their own nuclear weapons, that nonproliferation and disarmament are unrelated, and that the international community gives this nation little credit for its many nonproliferation and disarmament actions.

[…]

Endnotes

1 Presentations are available at https://www.ctbto.org/specials/ctbt-educational-resources/symposium-2016/recordingsof-sessions/.
2 https://www.ctbto.org/the-treaty/ctbt-ministerial-meetings/ctbt20ministerialmeeting/.
3 For treaty text and analysis, see U.S. Congress. Senate. Comprehensive Nuclear Test-Ban Treaty: Message from the President of the United States Transmitting Comprehensive Nuclear Test-Ban Treaty ... , Treaty Doc. 105-28, September 23, 1997. Washington: GPO, 1997, xvi + 230 p, http://www.gpo.gov/fdsys/pkg/CDOC-105tdoc28/pdf/ CDOC-105tdoc28.pdf, and U.S. Department of State. "Comprehensive Test Ban Treaty (CTBT)," http://www.state.gov/t/isn/trty/16411.htm
4 For a current list of signatures and ratifications, see "Status of Signature and Ratification" at the Comprehensive Nuclear Test-Ban-Treaty Organization website, http://www.ctbto.org/the-treaty/status-of-signature-and-ratification/.

GLOBAL VIEWPOINTS

CHAPTER 3

Nuclear Safety and
Security: Critical Issues

Nuclear Power Plants Are Vulnerable Targets

Karl Grossman

In the following viewpoint, Karl Grossman considers the nightmarish scenario of a terrorist attack on a nuclear power plant. Grossman refers to these as "pre-deployed weapons of mass destruction." A terrorist attack on a nuclear plant, however unlikely, would have devastating effects. Huge populations would be harmed or displaced, and massive environmental damage would ensue. Grossman argues that renewable energy provides green power, but with less risk. In particular, the abundant sunshine and political instability in the Middle East makes the region more suitable for solar power than nuclear. Grossman is professor of journalism at the State University of New York/College of New York and the author of the book, The Wrong Stuff: The Space's Program's Nuclear Threat to Our Planet.

As you read, consider the following questions:

1. Are nuclear power plants vulnerable? Why?
2. What evidence does the author provide to suggest an attack could target a nuclear plant?
3. According to the author, does the Nuclear Regulatory Commission (NRC) underestimate the current threat to nuclear power plants? Why or why not?

"Terrorism and nuclear power," by Karl Grossman, Enformable, March 31, 2016. Reprinted by permission.

P re-deployed weapons of mass destruction.

That's what nuclear power plants are. And that's another very big reason—demonstrated again in recent days with the disclosure that two of the Brussels terrorists were planning attacks on Belgian nuclear plants—why they must be eliminated.

Nuclear power plants are sitting ducks for terrorists. With most positioned along bays and rivers because of their need for massive amounts of coolant water, they provide a clear shot. They are fully exposed for aerial strikes.

The consequences of such an attack could far outweigh the impacts of 9/11 and, according to the U.S. 9/11 Commission, also originally considered in that attack was the use of hijacked planes to attack "unidentified nuclear power plants." The Indian Point nuclear plants 26 miles north of New York City were believed to be candidates.

As the Belgian newspaper Dernier Heure reported last week, regarding the plan to strike a Belgian nuclear plant, "investigators concluded that the target of terrorists was to 'jeopardize national security like never before.'"

The Union of Concerned Scientists in a statement on "Nuclear Security" declares:

> Terrorists pose a real and significant threat to nuclear power plants. The 2011 accident at Fukushima was a wake-up call reminding the world of the vulnerability of nuclear power plants to natural disasters such as earthquakes and floods. However, nature is not the only threat to nuclear facilities. They are inviting targets for sabotage and terrorist attack. A successful attack on a nuclear plant could have devastating consequences, killing, sickening or displacing large numbers of residents in the area surrounding the plant, and causing extensive long-time environmental damage.

A previously arranged "Nuclear Security Summit" is being held this week in Washington, D.C. with representatives of nations from around the world and with a focus on "nuclear terrorism."

Last week, in advance of the "summit" and in the wake of the Brussels suicide-bombings at the city's airport and a subway line, Yukiya Amano, director general of the International Atomic Energy Agency (IAEA), said: "Terrorism is spreading and the possibility of using nuclear material cannot be excluded. Member states need to have sustained interest in strengthening nuclear security. The countries which do not recognize the danger of nuclear terrorism is the biggest problem."

However, a main mission of the IAEA, ever since it was established by the UN in 1957 has been to promote nuclear power. It has dramatically minimized the consequences of the catastrophic accidents at Chernobyl and Fukushima and routinely understated all problems with atomic technology.

The "Nuclear Security Summit," with the IAEA playing a central role, is part of a series of gatherings following a speech made by President Barack Obama in Prague in 2009 in which he said "I am announcing a new international effort to secure all vulnerable nuclear material around the world."

In a press release this past August, White House spokesman Josh Earnest said this week's meeting "will continue discussion on the evolving [nuclear terrorism] threat and highlight steps that can be taken together to minimize the use of highly-enriched uranium, secure vulnerable materials, counter nuclear smuggling and deter, detect, and disrupt attempts at nuclear terrorism."

And, like the IAEA—formed as a result of a speech by U.S. President Dwight Eisenhower promoting "Atoms for Peace" at the UN—officials involved with nuclear power in the U.S. government and the nation's nuclear industry have long pushed atomic energy and downplayed problems about nuclear power and terrorism.

As the Union of Concerned Scientists (UCS) says in its "Nuclear Security" statement, "The adequacy of a security system depends on what we think we are protecting against. If we have underestimated the threat, we may overestimate our readiness to meet it. The NRC [U.S. Nuclear Regulatory Commission] has sometimes used unrealistically modest assumptions about potential attackers. The design basis threat (DBT) is the official definition of the security threats power plant management is required to protect against…. After 9/11, UCS criticized the DBT for nuclear plants on these grounds, among others."

UCS says the NRC "ignored the possibility of air-and water-based attacks…it did not address the possibility of large attacking groups using multiple entry points, or of an attack involving multiple insiders…it concentrated on threats to the reactor core, failing to address the vulnerability of spent fuel storage facilities." Since 2011, says the UCS, the NRC "finally revised its rules to address the threat of aircraft attack for new reactor designs—but at the same time has rejected proposed design changes to protect against water- and land-based attacks."

There is "also concern about the testing standard used," notes UCS. "In July 2012, the NRC adopted the new process. However, as a result of industry pressure, the standards were watered down."

Further, says UCS, testing is "currently required only for operating reactors, leaving questions about the adequacy of protection against attacks on reactors that have shut down, but still contain radioactive materials that could harm the public if damaged."

A pioneer in addressing how nuclear power plants are pre-deployed weapons of mass destruction has been Dr. Bennett Ramberg. As he wrote in his 1980 landmark book, *Nuclear Power Plants as Weapons for the Enemy: An Unrecognized Military Peril*, despite the "multiplication of nuclear power plants, little public consideration has been given to their vulnerability in time of war."

As he writes in a recent piece in *Foreign Affairs*, "Nuclear Power to the People: The Middle East's New Gold Rush," spotlighting the push now by many nations in the Middle East to build nuclear power plants, "Whatever the energy promise of the peaceful atom, evidently lost in the boom are the security risks inherent in setting up reactors in the Middle East—and not just the commonly voiced fear that reactors are harbingers of weapons. The real risk is the possibility that the plants themselves will become targets or hostages of nihilist Middle East militants, which could result in Chernobyl and Fukushima-like meltdowns."

"Given the mayhem that Islamic State (also called ISIS) and kindred groups have sown in the region and their end-of-days philosophy, the plausibility of an attempted attack on an operating nuclear power plant cannot be denied," writes Ramberg.

In fact, the plausibility of an attempted attack cannot be denied in the Middle East—or anywhere in world.

Says Ramberg: "If terrorists did strike a nuclear power plant in the Middle East, the nuclear fallout would depend on the integrity of reactors' own containment systems and the ability of emergency personnel to suppress the emissions, a difficult challenge for even the most advanced countries, as Japan found in Fukushima. Ongoing terrorism, civil strife, or war at the time the reactor is compromised would only complicate matters."

Moreover, he notes, "all nations in the Middle East share an increasingly practical alternative—solar energy."

Nations around the world, likewise, would be able to get along fine with solar, wind and differing mixes of other safe, clean, renewable energy—not susceptible to terrorist attack.

All 438 nuclear power plants around the world today could—and should—close now. The insignificant amount of electricity they generate—but 10 percent of total electric use—can be provided by other sources.

And green energy makes for a less costly power and a far safer world in comparison to catastrophic-danger prone and unnecessary nuclear power. We must welcome energy we can live with and reject power that presents a deadly threat in so many ways.

Nuclear Power Provides Safe, Reliable, and Clean Energy

Thomas J. Eiden

In the following viewpoint, Thomas J. Eiden defends nuclear power as a clean and efficient source of safe electricity. Eiden explains how nuclear fission plants work safely, citing the lower fatality rate of nuclear power as compared with other forms of energy such as coal and hydroelectric. While the risk of radioactive waste is often exaggerated, Eiden points out that nuclear waste actually has low levels of radioactivity. Moreover, modern reactors have several safety layers in place to prevent meltdowns such as the Chernobyl disaster. The piece is a polemic against regulators and environmental groups who delay construction of new plants and increase their already considerable capital outlay by causing interest to accrue. Eiden is a nuclear engineer for Battelle Energy Alliance and is a contributor to the Center for Industrial Progress.

As you read, consider the following questions:

1. What evidence does the author provide to make the case that nuclear power is safer than conventional forms of energy?
2. Why is an accident like Fukushima unlikely in a modern nuclear power plant?
3. Are safety regulations good or bad for the industry, according to this article?

"Nuclear Energy: The Safe, Clean, Cost-Effective Alternative," by Thomas J. Eiden, *The Objective Standard*. Reprinted by permission. Originally published in *The Objective Standard*, Vol.8, no.3, Fall 2013.

C ontrary to claims by opponents of nuclear energy that it is "unsafe," "unclean," and thus "unacceptable," nuclear energy is the safest, cleanest, and among the most practical forms of power generation today. Unfortunately, opponents of this wonderful source of power are succeeding in their efforts to deceive people about it; and the deceived, in turn, are fueling legislation and regulations that shackle the nuclear industry. It is time to set the record straight and to defend this life-serving industry. Let us begin with a summary of the nature of nuclear energy.

Nuclear power is generated by a controlled chain reaction involving the splitting of atoms. A modern nuclear power plant uses the intense heat created by this reaction to heat water and create steam, which turns a turbine and generates electricity. Whereas a coal-fired plant heats water by burning coal, a nuclear plant heats it by splitting atoms. This process is called nuclear fission.

Nuclear fission, in simple terms, occurs when an atom splits in two, releasing a massive amount of energy and several subatomic particles called neutrons. These neutrons, in turn, hit and split other atoms, beginning and sustaining the chain reaction. Reactor operators control this reaction in a variety of ways and thus regulate the amount of heat generated and energy produced.

The raw fuel for this process is the metal uranium, which must be enriched before it can be used for producing energy in commercial reactors. Enrichment is necessary because mined uranium ore is around 99.3 percent uranium-238, which, in today's commercial power plants, does not readily split upon exposure to neutrons from the fission chain reaction, and thus makes poor fuel. The other 0.7 percent of mined uranium is uranium-235, which makes excellent fuel. The number refers to the atomic mass, or the total mass of protons and neutrons that make up the atomic nucleus. This difference in mass of the same element makes them two different isotopes of uranium. The enrichment process consists essentially of increasing the percentage of uranium-235 by decreasing the percentage (via removal) of uranium-238.

The fuel manufacturing process ultimately yields black, pinky-sized pellets of usable nuclear fuel. These pellets are stacked in tubes of a special metal alloy, and thousands of these fuel rods are placed in a reactor core. The rods are arranged in a very specific geometric configuration to enable a sustained nuclear reaction to occur. The nuclear fission reaction is controlled by inserting or removing a separate set of rods made of neutron-absorbing metal or by adding neutron-absorbing chemicals to the water that cools the reactor.

All methods of producing energy involve risk, and nuclear fission is no exception. Historically, however, nuclear power has been by far the safest form of energy production among reliable and scalable energy sources.

Nuclear power is safer than other forms of energy for several reasons. To begin with, multiple layers of safety mechanisms and precautions are built into nuclear power plants. For instance, if a nuclear power plant is completely cut off from the electrical grid during an accident, backup generators automatically start to power safety systems that continue to cool the reactor. If the generators fail, secondary backups such as battery banks are deployed. In case of an earthquake or a seismic event beyond a certain magnitude, nuclear plants automatically shut down. New plant designs currently under construction use circulating air and water moved by the heat of the core itself to cool the shut-down reactor, which means the safety system does not require human intervention or even power to operate for sustained periods.[1] And massive, immensely fortified containment domes are hallmarks of nuclear power plants. In the extremely rare event that radioactive material leaks from the core of a modern power plant, a dome serves to contain it.

During a severe accident scenario or natural disaster involving a nuclear reactor, the event typically unfolds over hours or even days, enabling engineers and operators to react as necessary and mitigate damage. Few types of industrial accidents enable such long periods for corrective action, containment, or, in the rare case it is necessary, evacuation. If a construction crew accidentally ruptures an underground natural gas line with a backhoe and it explodes, the whole event occurs in a fraction of a second. If a coal mine caves in, the whole event might take several seconds, perhaps a minute. Likewise if a hydroelectric dam breaks.

Of course, the production of energy by any means can be dangerous, and like any toxic or combustible materials, radioactive materials must be handled with care. But the technology and advanced reactor designs scientists and engineers have developed in recent decades render catastrophes practically impossible. And, of course, reactors get safer and safer as technology advances and designs improve. Currently, it is beyond doubt that modern nuclear reactors are far and away the safest of the energy alternatives.

The chart below compares the number of fatalities from various forms of energy production. Accurate comparison is made possible by viewing the number of deaths per terawatt-year (TWy).[2]

Comparison of Accident Statistics in Energy Production, 1970–1992[3]

FUEL	IMMEDIATE FATALITIES 1970–92	DEMOGRAPHIC	NORMALIZED TO DEATHS PER TWY ELECTRICITY
Coal	6,400	Workers	342
Natural Gas	1,200	Workers & Public	85
Hydroelectric	4,000	Public	883
Nuclear	31	Workers	8

Nuclear power plants also create very little waste compared to other forms of energy generation and emit no air pollution. Because nothing is burned or leaves the core during the nuclear fission process, the only emission from a nuclear plant is steam or hot water. When the fuel is removed, it comes out of the core looking identical to when it was put in: a metal assembly containing nuclear fuel pellets—not some glowing, green ooze, as works of fiction would have us believe. The only difference is that about

5 percent of the uranium-235 has been spent, and the fuel no longer contains enough of it to sustain the nuclear chain reaction. Used fuel assemblies are stored and cooled in pools of water outside of the core (but still in the plant) to let highly radioactive materials decay. Later the used fuel assemblies are removed from the pools and stored in steel-lined concrete casks.

All of the nuclear waste produced in the past forty years by commercial nuclear power plants in the United States can be stacked in the space of a football field and only seven yards high.[4] If these nuclear plants were solar plants of comparable electrical output, the volume of waste would be some sixty-three thousand times greater,[5] as solar panels contain glass and toxic metals that need to be safely disposed of after their operational life.

The waste generated by nuclear power is extremely compact because of the energy density of nuclear fuel. A small volume of purified uranium packs enormous potential energy: A one-gram pellet has potential energy equal to 2.8 tons of coal or six hundred gallons of oil.[6] This is why, in addition to creating a relatively miniscule amount of waste, nuclear reactors can run continuously for up to eighteen months without refueling.

The amount of usable uranium accessible by today's standard technology could power the industrial world for thousands of years. With technological advances, nuclear power easily could provide the world's energy needs for millions of years. By finding more and better ways to extract uranium (e.g., extracting it from seawater), by recycling used fuel, and by building special reactors to use and reuse nuclear waste, the power this technology can provide has no end. And that does not even account for the potential involved in developing reactors that use non-uranium nuclear fuels, such as thorium, which is many times more abundant than uranium.

Despite the advancements in nuclear power over the past sixty years, a number of falsehoods about the technology persist. So let us address and dispel some of these here.

Because nuclear power involves highly complex physics and engineering, people with little or no understanding of these fields can be and often are confused or misled about it. For example, without an understanding of the nature and process of radioactive decay, one might be led to believe that all radioactive materials are equally and forever toxic. But this is not the case. Although some components of nuclear waste are radioactive for thousands of years, these materials are not very radioactive, and they are much less toxic than radioactive materials that decay quickly. As a rule, radioactive materials that take a long time to decay are by that fact not highly radioactive.

People are also frequently misled to the effect that "there is no safe dose of radiation" or "an explosion at a nuclear power plant can kill thousands of people." (Such claims are sometimes accompanied by pictures of people who have been poisoned by radiation or mushroom clouds from nuclear bombs.) Environmentalist groups such as Greenpeace, Sierra Club, and the Natural Resource Defense Council (NRDC) have a long track record of spreading such falsehoods while campaigning against nuclear power. (They use the same tactics to campaign against fossil fuels.)

Greenpeace, for example, released a "fact sheet" on radiation that, far from clarifying matters or enlightening people about nuclear power, muddles the issues with the obvious aim of terrifying people. Concerning radiation exposure, Greenpeace says:

> There is no safe dose of radiation. Radiation doses need to be kept as low as possible. Internationally accepted limits are set for members of the public for doses that are in addition to background or natural radiation. The limit is set at one millisievert a year. For nuclear workers, this limit is 20 millisieverts a year. To compare, the global average for natural radiation doses is 2.4 millisieverts a year.[7]

This is a scare tactic. The so-called "internationally accepted limit" of one millisievert per year is about the same amount of radiation that Grand Central Station employees receive each year from the granite walls of the station. Even the rules of the Nuclear Regularity Commission (NRC) concerning professions involving radiation—such as nuclear power plant workers and medical staff who handle radioactive medicine or operate radiation-producing equipment—permit workers to receive up to fifty millisieverts of radiation per year. (Workers, however, rarely receive anything near that.)

We all get around three to four millisieverts of radiation per year by such means as traveling in planes, living in brick houses, or residing at higher elevations (such as Denver, Colorado). Our sun is a giant nuclear fusion reactor, so, naturally, being closer to it or being exposed to sunlight more often exposes a person to more radiation. So does receiving an X-ray or using a tanning lamp. So does eating Brazil nuts or bananas. We regularly receive "background" doses of radiation because radiation is practically everywhere. If, as Greenpeace claims, "there is no safe dose of radiation," then there is no safe place to be.

Modern scientific observations show that doses of radiation under a certain threshold have no discernible negative health effects. In parts of the world—such as Ramsar, Iran, and Guarapari, Brazil—where people receive larger annual doses of background radiation than most nuclear plant technicians receive, cancer rates have shown no statistical increase.[8] But such facts have no effect on the likes of Greenpeace.

Next, consider the ridiculous implications that a nuclear power plant can explode like a nuclear bomb. This is physically impossible. To begin with, in order to explode, nuclear material must be enriched to more than 95 percent uranium-235, and fuel is only around 3 percent uranium-235. Further, in order to explode, the uranium would have to be shaped in a very specific way—and then intentionally triggered. No one with even a smidgen of understanding of the nature of nuclear energy can honestly suggest or imply that a nuclear reactor core can explode like a nuclear bomb. But that doesn't stop antinuclear zealots from pretending otherwise and terrifying people in the process.

The Sierra Club has a "fact sheet" similar to that of Greenpeace. The Sierra Club's fiction begins: "As the disasters at Chernobyl, Three Mile Island and Fukushima have shown, nuclear power can cause catastrophic damage to land, human health, and our food supply."[9] That is an intentional grouping of wildly dissimilar things. The Chernobyl accident—which occurred under the Soviet political regime and could never be repeated with modern plants in the West—was a disaster and did result in immediate fatalities to many plant workers. It also appears to have caused a large increase in thyroid cancer due to people unknowingly ingesting food contaminated by the radiation.[10] (Fortunately, the vast majority of these cases were treatable.)

The events at Three Mile Island and Fukushima, however, were different matters altogether. These incidents were testaments not to the danger but to the safety of nuclear power plants. Zero people died as a result of the problems at these plants.

The Three Mile Island accident originated when a valve became stuck open and began to drain coolant from one of the reactors. This situation, combined with the fact that plant operators mistakenly thought too much coolant was flowing in, led operators to remove even more coolant. Eventually, the reactor core became too hot, and the fuel melted but did not leak from the steel pressure vessel that contains the core. However, during the initial confusion, operators intentionally released a very small quantity of radioactive steam. Even so, the accident did not (significantly) contaminate surrounding land, nor did it have any impact on human health.[11] The power plant continues to operate to this day with its other reactor core, and valuable information was gleaned from the incident on how a reactor handles a meltdown, the "worst-case scenario."

The incident at the Fukushima-Daiichi power plant was caused by an immense natural disaster involving a massive earthquake and a huge tsunami. The power plant is located on the coast, where it used ocean water to cool its reactors. When the earthquake occurred, it triggered the automatic shutdown of the reactors, but the tsunami that followed destroyed most of the electrical equipment in the plant as well as infrastructure as far as several miles inland. The plant's backup generators were flooded with water, and the plant was cut off from the electrical grid. A third backup battery system kicked in but eventually ran out of power. With no power to pump water to remove the remaining heat, some of the reactor cores melted.

The meltdown at Fukushima released some radioactive material, mostly in the form of contaminated vented steam or dust, but the released material was and is monitored and tracked (the current status can be checked on interactive maps online).[12] The meltdown at Fukushima did not kill anyone or destroy large swaths of land. Some people died from the stress of the disaster, and others from being abandoned in nearby hospitals or retirement homes when their staff fled the buildings unnecessarily.[13] But no one died from radiation exposure.

Some land around the plant and downwind from it was contaminated, and the cleanup will be costly. Some seawater around the plant was contaminated as well. However, much of the area in the evacuation zone around the plant is safe, and people are already returning to their homes.

Another important difference between the Chernobyl plant in the socialist Ukraine and modern plants in relatively civilized countries is the surrounding legal and political context. Civilized countries such as the United States and Japan have legal structures in place that protect rights and punish negligence. In the United States, if a person or a company or the government contaminates your land or property, you can sue him or it for damages. In the socialist Ukraine, there were no such provisions—certainly not with respect to the government. The Chernobyl power plant was an inherently unstable design, and negligent and unaccountable government operators pushed it beyond its limits.

In short, the legal, economic, and technical environments pertaining to the problems at Three Mile Island and Fukushima were completely different than those pertaining to the disaster at Chernobyl. But this doesn't stop antinuclear zealots from pretending otherwise.

Some of the same groups that dishonestly demonize nuclear power also litigate against it. Organizations such as the Natural Resource Defense Council use litigation to thwart progress and distort facts concerning nuclear energy.[14] For example, the NRDC and sundry environmentalist groups file mendacious lawsuits against utilities and thus delay licensing and construction of those facilities.[15] Because nuclear plants are extremely capital-intensive projects—especially given all the safety precautions involved—delays in construction incur (among other expenses) huge interest penalties on loans utilities have taken out to finance construction. After delaying construction by such means, the NRDC has the audacity to claim on its "fact sheet" that nuclear power entails high construction costs and is uneconomical. The fact is that existing nuclear plants deliver energy at prices competitive with every source of reliable energy.[16] The big difference is that nuclear power is much safer and cleaner than the alternatives. But the facts don't make the NRDC's "fact sheet."

The NRDC's fiction continues, claiming "New nuclear power plants are unlikely to provide a significant fraction of future U.S. needs for low-carbon energy."[17] This claim is made in full light of the fact that existing nuclear plants provide about 20 percent of the electricity used in the United States today.[18]

Despite the demonstrable cleanliness, safety, and efficiency of nuclear power—and despite the fact that the fuel for it is virtually unlimited—opposition to this life-serving technology rages on; consequently, myriad regulations are stifling the industry. Much of this opposition and many of these regulations are inspired and perpetuated by the false claims of antinuclear and environmentalist groups.

Compliance with regulations is extremely expensive, and the number of controls on the nuclear industry is only increasing, raising the cost of nuclear power far beyond what it would be in a substantially freer market.[19]

Partly due to the scientifically absurd notion that nuclear power is an existential threat to mankind, the government has created a dedicated regulatory body, the Nuclear Regulatory Commission, to police the industry. The NRC is involved in every step of the process of conceiving, building, and operating a nuclear power plant—requiring myriad licenses, permissions, inspections, and the like. These controls and regulations can cost a utility several hundred million dollars just to get a nuclear power plant up and running.[20]

In some cases, local and state governments are actively trying to shut down nuclear plants, even when it means economic suicide for the region. In Vermont, for instance, where the Vermont Yankee Nuclear Plant provides 70 percent of the state's electricity, the utility that owns Vermont Yankee had to fight a protracted legal battle with the Vermont state government in order to continue producing electricity for the region.[21]

When environmentalist groups don't get their way through legislation or litigation, many resort to more brutish tactics. Environmentalist groups have a long history of using direct physical force to throttle or thwart industry, from chaining themselves to equipment,[22] to climbing cooling towers, to creating human blockades at a plant's front gate or a construction site,[23] to laying their (mindless) bodies across railroad tracks.[24]

Nuclear power is one of the greatest, most life-serving advancements since the control of fire. Yet the nuclear industry and the men and women who deliver or attempt to deliver nuclear energy are attacked and shackled for their efforts. Those who advocate and would tighten the shackles either do not understand what nuclear power is and how it works—or they do understand but intentionally misrepresent it. Either way, they are engaging in a gross injustice against the heroic scientists, engineers, and businessmen who seek to deliver and advance nuclear power, and against everyone on the planet who benefits or could benefit from the technology—which means everyone on the planet.

It is time to unshackle this industry, its minds, its businesses, and its potential to enhance human life. It is time to recognize nuclear power as the clean, safe, economical source of energy that it is. It is time to recognize this good for being good.

Endnotes

1 "Plant Vogtle Units 3 and 4," Georgia Power, http://www.southerncompany.com/what-doing/energy-innovation/nuclear-energy/pdfs/vogtle-nuclear-brochure.pdf (accessed July 26, 2013).

2 A terawatt-year is 8.76 x 1012 kilowatt-hours. For a further description, see "Energy Units," American Physical Society, 2013, http://www.aps.org/policy/reports/popa-reports/energy/units.cfm.

3 "Environment and Health in Electricity Generation," World Nuclear Association, December 2012, http://www.world-nuclear.org/education/ehs.html.

4 "Nuclear Waste: Amounts and On-Site Storage," Nuclear Energy Institute, http://www.nei.org/resourcesandstats/nuclear_statistics/nuclearwasteamountsandonsitestorage/ (accessed December 20, 2012).

5 "The Real Waste Problem, Solar Edition," Things Worse Than Nuclear Power, http://www.thingsworsethannuclearpower.com/2012/09/the-real-waste-problem-solar-edition.html (accessed April 27, 2013).

6 Thomas Eiden, "Energy Density of Uranium," Power for Progress, January 18, 2013, http://thomaseiden.com/index.php/energy-density-of-uranium/.

7 "Radiation," Greenpeace International, February 2012, http://www.greenpeace.org/usa/PageFiles/391730/Radiation.pdf.

8 S. M. J. Mortazavi and H. Mozdarani, "Non-Linear Phenomena in Biological Findings of the Residents of High Background Radiation Areas of Ramsar," *International Journal of Radiation Research*, January 2013, vol. 11, no. 1, http://www.academia.edu/3390583/Non-linear_phenomena_in_biological_findings_of_the_residents_of_high_background_radiation_areas_of_Ramsar.

9 "Nuclear Facts," Sierra Club, http://www.sierraclub.org/nuclear/factsheet.aspx (accessed December 20, 2012).

10 "Health Effects of the Chernobyl Accident: An Overview," World Health Organization, April 2006, http://www.who.int/ionizing_radiation/chernobyl/backgrounder/en/index.html.

11 "Backgrounder on the Three Mile Island Accident," Nuclear Regulatory Commission, February 11, 2013, http://www.nrc.gov/reading-rm/doc-collections/fact-sheets/3mile-isle.html.

12 "Japan Radiation Map," Institute for Information Design, http://jciv.iidj.net/map/ (accessed July 30, 2013).

13 "Old People Suffer Abandonment, Cold in Wake of Tsunami," NBC News, March 18, 2011, http://www.msnbc.msn.com/id/42150705/ns/world_news-asia_pacific/t/old-people-suffer-abandonment-cold-wake-tsunami/.

14 "NRDC: Litigation Team," Natural Resources Defense Council, http://www.nrdc.org/about/staff/litigation.asp (accessed April 5, 2013). "U.S. Nuclear Regulatory Commission Halts Nuclear Reactor Licensing Decisions in Response to NRDC Lawsuit," Natural Resources Defense Council, August 14, 2012, http://www.nrdc.org/nuclear/NRC-waste-confidence-decision.asp.

15 Kristi E. Swartz, "Groups Sue to Stop Vogtle Expansion Project," *Atlanta Journal Constitution*, February 16, 2012, http://www.ajc.com/news/business/groups-sue-to-stop-vogtle-expansion-project/nQRN3/; "Vermont Yankee Nuclear Power Corp. v. Natural Resources Defense Council," *Environmental Law Reporter*, http://elr.info/litigation/%5Bfield_article_volume-raw%5D/20288/vermont-yankee-nuclear-power-corp-v-natural-resources-de (accessed August 1, 2013).

16 "Electric Power Annual," U.S. Energy Information Administration, http://www.eia.gov/electricity/annual/html/epa_08_04.html (accessed April 28, 2013).

17 "NRDC: Renewable Energy for America: Technologies," Natural Resources Defense Council, http://www.nrdc.org/energy/renewables/technologies.asp (accessed December 20, 2012).

18 "Nuclear Power in the USA," World Nuclear Association, April 2013, http://www.world-nuclear.org/info/Country-Profiles/Countries-T-Z/USA–Nuclear-Power/#.UV6SlpM2bzw.

19 Bernard Cohen, *Costs of Nuclear Power Plants—What Went Wrong?* (New York: Plenum Press, 1990), http://www.phyast.pitt.edu/~blc/book/chapter9.html.

20 "mPower Empowered by SMR Funds," *World Nuclear News*, November 12, 2012, http://www.world-nuclear-news.org/NN-mPower_empowered_by_SMR_funds_121112a.html; "NRC: Fact Sheet on Reactor License Renewal," U.S. NRC, June 19, 2012, http://www.nrc.gov/reading-rm/doc-collections/fact-sheets/fs-reactor-license-renewal.html.

21 "Vermont Yankee Wins Right to Keep Generating," *World Nuclear News*, January 20, 2012, http://www.world-nuclear-news.org/RS_Vermont_Yankee_wins_right_to_keep_generating_200112a.html.

22 "Anti-nuclear Protests in the United States," Wikipedia, http://en.wikipedia.org/w/index.php?title=Anti-nuclear_protests_in_the_United_States&oldid=548634094.

23 "Environment: The Siege of Seabrook," *Time*, May 16, 1977, http://www.time.com/time/magazine/article/0,9171,918965,00.html.

24 "German Nuclear Protest Halts Train," Mail Online, http://www.dailymail.co.uk/news/article-34011/German-nuclear-protest-halts-train.html (accessed July 21, 2013).

In Japan, Fukushima Proved Nuclear Power to Be Safer than People Thought

Kelvin Kemm

In the following viewpoint, Kelvin Kemm argues that contrary to conventional wisdom, the Fukushima nuclear disaster in Japan actually proves that nuclear power is safe. Kemm likens the accident to a crash test, and since no fatalities occurred, he concludes that the plant passed with high marks. Indeed, the only reason it failed was because of outdoor diesel tanks for the backup generators. Although it is true that Fukushima could have been worse, the long-term damage to the Pacific Oceancaused by radioactive material has yet to be assessed accurately. Kemm is the CEO of Nuclear Africa and a member of the International Board of Advisors of CFACT. Dr. Kemm received the prestigious Lifetime Achievers Award of the National Science and Technology Forum of South Africa.

As you read, consider the following questions:

1. What is the main "lesson of Fukushima" according to the author?
2. What were the results of the United Nations (UNSCEAR) inspection?
3. How does the author suggest radioactivity is misunderstood?

"The lesson of Fukushima—Nuclear energy is safe," by Kelvin Kemm, CFACT, February 16, 2015. Reprinted by permission.

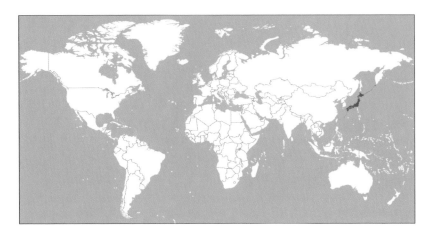

W e often hear and read the phrase "The lessons learned from Fukushima."

The phrase is frequently spoken in sombre tone, accompanied by knowing looks and the shaking of heads.

So what were the lessons learned from Fukushima? Quite simply they are that nuclear power has been proven to be much safer than anyone previously imagined.

The nuclear fraternity worldwide should have celebrated after the Fukushima drama. The world watched the entire saga, second by second…and what was the outcome?

Answer: total people killed by radiation, zero. Total injured, zero. Total private property damaged by radiation, zero. Expected long term effects on people; zero.

If scientists had wanted to design an intentional 'crash experiment' as is done with motor cars in crash labs, there could not have been a better one than the reality which unfolded at Fukushima. A forty year old nuclear power plant, built to a sixty year old design, was struck by the largest earthquake on record. The reactors survived that with no problem. They shut down as designed. Then, 55 minutes later, the largest Tsunami on record arrived. The giant wall of water jumped the protective wall, and slammed into the nuclear plant. The plant survived that too…

initially. But then previous bad management decisions came into play, like ghosts from the past.

Years earlier it had been decided to place the back-up diesel fuel tanks outdoors. Bad decision!

These tanks held the reserve fuel for the emergency diesel cooling pumps, to be used if and when the primary electrical pumps failed. The tsunami washed away the power lines supplying the electricity to the primary reactor cooling pumps…so they needed the diesel pumps…fast.

No fuel, it was all floating away with the rest of the debris from the smashed up houses, schools, police station, airport, shops, offices, harbour…you get the picture. The roads were gone, or blocked with debris; so no police, fire brigade, army units, were coming in to help.

The reactors all shut down correctly, no problem there, but hot reactor fuel needs to be water-cooled for two to five days after an emergency shutdown, to remove residual heat. In nuclear jargon this is known as "decay heat." So the reactor engineers started to work, with their backs to the wall, with no pumps and no help; the world was watching; and top management was yelling for fast answers. The whole scene, like a theatrical drama, could not have been worse.

As I said: if a scientific team had intentionally designed a lab crash test for a nuclear power plant, they could not have done better than the reality of Fukushima Daiichi.

In spite of this whole theatrical drama the result was…nobody killed or injured, and no indication of long term negative radiation effects on people. So the lesson of Fukushima is that nuclear power is much safer than people thought.

In April 2014, the Japanese government allowed the civilian population to return to the district of Miyakoji near Fukushima. In early 2013 the area had already been declared safe, from a radiological point of view, but the damage caused by the tsunami still had to be repaired; such as water supplies, sewerage, roads and so on.

This rebuilding of infrastructure was started in mid 2013. Rice was planted in May 2013.

People started returning incrementally, as they got their own houses operational again. In April local shops opened, refuse collection restarted and a health clinic and children's play centre opened. A tourist attraction, the Tokiwa Sky Palace, opened for business as usual. Obviously it must be a very emotional experience to return to your home after a devastating tsunami has swept the area. The TV images of the surging water were horrific. Part of the elevated freeway near Miyakoji collapsed as a result of the tsunami, and the Japanese Prime Minister Shinzo Abe has said that it will still take a couple of years to rebuild the road, so residents will have to make alternative plans in the meantime.

The world still watches Fukushima with morbid fascination. Strangely, the world media does not seem too concerned with the more than 15,000 people killed by the tsunami, or with the massive swathes of residential and industrial property pulverized by the tons of debris propelled by the mighty tsunami waters, like an armada of water-borne bulldozers.

Instead they watched the Fukushima plant workers fill hundreds of large water tanks with run off rain water and other waste water from the power station site. The water is labelled "radioactive."

In reality, this water is so mildly radioactive that if a person drank nothing but that water for three months it would equal the radiation ingested by eating one restaurant portion of tuna.

Many people do not seem to realise that radiation is around all people all of the time. Natural radiation is constantly streaming down onto planet earth from the stars. The stars are all giant nuclear reactors. Radiation is also constantly coming up from the ground. This comes from the residual radiation in the earth, dating from when the earth cooled from a ball of molten goo, which included many radioactive elements.

Production Costs* of U.S. Electricity
*production costs = operation and maintenance + fuel

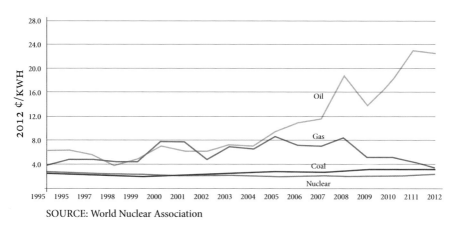

SOURCE: World Nuclear Association

United Nations Inspection

In January 2013 the United Nations Scientific Committee on the Effects of Atomic Radiation (UNSCEAR), was asked by the UN General Assembly to carry out a comprehensive study of the "full assessment of the levels of exposure and radiation risks" to the people around Fukushima.

After two years of study UNSCEAR released its report which stated that rates of cancer, or hereditary diseases, were unlikely to show any discernible rise in the affected areas, because the radiation doses received by people were just too low.

In general, people living in the vicinity of Fukushima are expected to accumulate an additional lifetime dose of less than 10 mSv, compared to an average lifetime dose of 170 mSv for the average Japanese citizen, as received from all natural sources.

UNSCEAR also stated: "No discernible increased incidence of radiation-related health effects are expected among exposed members of the public or their descendants."

The Head of the World Nuclear Association, Agneta Rising, said that the UNSCEAR report "should greatly reassure those thinking of returning to evacuated areas."

She added: "Experience has taught us that some measures to prevent radiation dose can be more damaging than the doses avoided. They also exacerbate fears that lead to social and economic suffering. We need practical measures for protecting people that also help them get on with their lives when the emergency is over."

UNSCEAR also said that the potential for radiation effects in the wider Pacific Ocean are "insignificant." The scare mongers on the other hand, have reported claims of dead fish visible right across the Pacific Ocean, and even US navy sailors getting ill from radiation on an aircraft carrier. A video clip on the internet shows sailors sweeping a thick soap foam off the carrier flight deck, while the anti-nuclear commentary refers to radioactive ash, as if the visible while soap foam was actually radioactive ash.

The Other Fukushima

It is also instructive to note that there are two Fukushima nuclear power plants; Fukushima Daiichi and Fukushima Daini. Daiichi, meaning "number two" was the one the world watched; Daini, meaning "number one" fought its own battles, virtually unnoticed.

Fukushima Daini is 10 km to the south of Daiichi and it was also hit by the tsunami, which was far larger than Daini was designed for. In stark contrast to Daiichi, Daini withstood the onslaught with one power line and one diesel generator still intact. That made all the difference! The Daini operators also battled huge odds, with three of their four reactors lacking sufficient cooling power. But as a few days passed, the skilful operators were able to bring all the reactors to a state of cold shutdown, without radiation release, and without the major damage suffered at Daiichi.

So the Daini saga was a very interesting "control comparison" which unfolded in parallel to the main drama, which played out only 10km away.

The Dose Counts

During the past century of nuclear technology worldwide, no harm whatsoever has ever been detected in any person who received a radiation dose of less than 100 mSv in a very short space of time.

In fact, no harm has been detected as a result of doses more than twice that figure. Because nuclear radiation is itself an energy source, it is extremely easy to detect in extremely small quantities, so very mild radiation can easily be detected around Fukushima. It is of no health consequence to anybody. The only harm which is real is the public relations image harm to the Japanese government and the Management of TEPCO who spend their time apologising and falling over their own feet, rather than being scientifically realistic.

People worry about "migration through the soil" and radiation getting into underground water, or into the sea. These mental images sound mysterious and scary, but reality is different.

Interestingly, the oldest nuclear reactors in the world are in Africa. They are more than 1.5 billion years old. They are natural reactors in the ground at a place in Gabon called Oklo and were discovered in 1972. Way back in geological time bacteria in some swampy ponds interacted with metals in the ground and caused natural uranium to concentrate in the ponds. The ratios of the uranium isotopes back then made it possible for a natural nuclear reaction to start in the ground, in the presence of water.

The operating natural reactors would have heated up and produced nuclear waste. They probably boiled off the water, over some period of time, and stopped working, until more water arrived, and so the cycle would have gone on until the fissionable uranium was largely used.

The French received a great surprise when they started mining uranium there in the 1970's. They sent samples back to France and on analysis it was found that the uranium was depleted in the fissionable isotope—the portion needed to run nuclear power plants. They were amazed. This should have not been possible.

It looked like the Oklo uranium was conventional depleted uranium which had come out of an operating nuclear plant. On

Radiation Doses and Limits

■ Dose Limit from NRC-licensed activity

■ Radiation Doses

5,000
Annual Nuclear Worker Dose Limit (NRC)

1,000
Whole Body CT

620
Average US Annual Dose

310
US Avg Natural Background Dose

100
Annual Public Dose Limit (NRC)

40
From Your Body

30
Cosmic Rays

10
Chest X-Ray

4
Safe Drinking Water Limit (EPA)

2.5
Trans-Atlantic Flight

SOURCE: Nuclear Regulatory Commission

further investigation this turned out to be exactly the case. The Oklo reactors had run as natural reactors in the ground for very many years.

There is no sign of any nuclear radiation damage to any fauna and flora in the area, despite very many years of unhindered nuclear isotope migration.

Radiation Reality

We now need to take a moment to ponder what radiation actually is; and when and how it may be dangerous.

Imagine that you are in a room and that a radioactive brick is on the table on the other side of the room. If the total dose that you would receive from the brick, by being in the room, is less than about 100 mSv then it matters not the slighted that you would sit in the room with the radioactive brick. In fact you can eat your lunch without any concern.

When you go home and walk out of the room, and close the door, the radiation falling on you is gone, totally. When you go home you are carrying no radiation whatsoever, and you are 100% safe.

The further you walk away from a source of radiation the weaker it gets, very rapidly. The dose received can be compared to that of light. As you walk away from a glowing light bulb the amount of light falling on you decreases fast. Same with radiation coming from a single source.

Now we come to the term, radioactive 'contamination' which historically was a bad choice of term, but we have to live with it now. If my mythical radioactive brick was ground up into fine powder and then put in a bowl in the room, together with an electric fan we would have radioactive dust flying about and landing on everything, including you and your lunch.

The chair, table, carpet, lunchbox are all then said to be "contaminated" with radioactive dust. "Contamination" is fine mobile radioactive material like dust.

When the dust lands on your clothes you would not be permitted to go home with the clothes, carrying the dust. You would have to take all the clothes off and have a shower and a good scrub. A Geiger counter would then be used to determine if any dust were still on you.

When the radiation inspector deemed you to be 'clean' you would be allowed to go home…wearing some other clothes, because your dust laden clothes would be buried in a nuclear waste repository, according to a legally verified nuclear waste processing protocol. You could go home, having had a fright, but being perfectly safe.

However, if the radioactive dust landed on your lunch, and you then ate it, you would have a potential problem because the radioactive material would be inside you and then can't easily be 'washed away.'

Worse still would be if you had got a great surprise to see all the radioactive dust swirling around and you had taken a great gasp and sucked the radioactive dust into your lungs.

The dust in your stomach would mostly pass right through your gut and then out in a couple of days, presenting a reasonably minor risk. Radioactive dust in lungs is a different matter.

Even dust in lungs would mostly be ejected by the normal bodily lung cleaning mechanism, but a very small amount could get stuck in the lung lining for years. It is this dust, stuck in one place, slowly irritating one spot for years, which can lead to the nucleation of a cancer.

So, by far the greatest human danger resulting from any release from an accident such as Fukushima, is mobile radiation, usually dust, which is known as contamination. Breathing in radioactive contamination is much worse than eating it.

If somebody were to go home with radioactive dust on their clothes and then hug their child, the child could breathe in the dust. That is why the authorities worry so much about contamination and so cordon off areas. They worry about wind direction, or vehicles leaving the scene which could carry dust.

That is why the nuclear plant workers sometimes wear those spaceman-like suits; to stop dust getting on them, not to stop radiation.

Gama radiation will go clean through those suits. The suits stay behind when the worker goes home.

Fear and Pressure

As the residents of the Fukushima region return to their homes one really does have to ask: what were the lessons learned?

One is that nuclear was shown to be extremely safe. But another is; that far more needs to be done to educate the public and the authorities about the true nature of nuclear power and nuclear radiation.

The Japanese authorities completely overreacted by removing so many people from their homes around Fukushima. The residents suffered huge trauma as a result of the forced evacuations. They would have been much safer staying in their homes. No doubt, media pressure and associated world public scare played a major role in inducing the Japanese authorities to act the way they did.

It is currently playing a role in causing the Japanese authorities to continue acting the way they are. They should rather be using science and not superstition.

Hopefully as time passes, the real truth of Fukushima will be recorded in history and not the knee-jerk scares which have tended to gain centre stage.

In Japan, Nuclear Opponents Exploit Fukushima Accident in Spite of Evidence

Willem Post

In the following viewpoint, Willem Post counters those who might use the Fukushima disaster to exaggerate the risks of nuclear power. While the tsunami itself and resulting evacuation caused horrendous casualties, Post argues that the deaths directly attributable to Fukushima are extremely low. This is the case, even including estimated cancer deaths over the next 130 years. The article also cites statistics that show the probable death rates had Japan been using coal, oil, and gas for power rather than nuclear energy. From these data, the author concludes that nuclear power is still comparatively safe, even taking into account the aftermath of Fukushima. Post is a consulting engineer specializing in energy efficiency of buildings and building systems.

As you read, consider the following questions:

1. How has Fukushima impacted Japan's economy?
2. Why does the author claim that damage from Fukushima was mostly psychological?
3. How is radiation risk from Fukushima assessed in this viewpoint?

"Deaths from Nuclear Energy Compared with Other Causes," by Willem Post, Energy Post Productions B.V., February 26, 2013. Reprinted by permission.

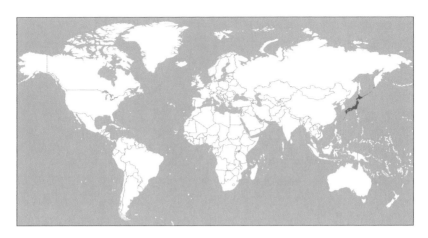

My first reaction to the aerial photos of Fukushima power plant site was: why did they put the auxiliary transformers, that provide power to the plant, and the emergency diesel-generators, that provide power to the auxiliary transformers, on the OCEAN side? They should have been on the land side, protected from earthquakes, and out of reach of any tsunami.

The lack of emergency power to operate the cooling pumps caused the reactor cores to overheat, melt and evaporate and the pressure vessel to crack. Gases released inside the concrete building caused an explosion blowing out the walls and roofs.

The result of the tsunami was much loss of life, extensive property damage, social and economic stress and an economic recession.

To offset the loss of electrical energy production, Japan needed to import more fossil fuels, mostly high-cost LNG, that caused its balance of payments surplus to be reduced, as the products made with the more expensive energy became less competitive.

It is useful to look at the present and predicted future loss of life of the Fukushima events and compare it to other causes of loss of life to place matters in perspective, and to reduce opportunities for some people to take advantage for self-serving purposes.

For example: The self-serving, scare-mongering by various global warming/climate change activists and promoters of renewable energy regarding the dangers of nuclear energy shows itself to be irrational after comparing some real-life numbers.

Fukushima

Radiation Measurements
Readings of radiation were taken during the June 6–July 7 period. The values shown on the below map are in nanoSieverts/hr.

The highest readings are 6,400 nSv/hr, or 8,760 x 6,400 = 56,064,000 nano Sv/yr = 56 milliSv/yr, about 15 – 20 times background. The two purple dots close to the plant indicate 19,000 nSv/hr and 206,000 nSv/hr. People were exposed to these levels for a few hours, or a few days, until being evacuated.

http://jciv.iidj.net/map/fukushima/

Deaths and Adverse Health Effects To-Date
Up till now, no one has died of radiation exposure. The main adverse health effects due to the Fukushima accident have been psychological.

Kazuo Sakai of Japan's National Institute of Radiological Sciences said:

> Since the accident in Fukushima, no health effects from radiation have been observed, although we have heard reports some people fell ill due to stress from living as evacuees and due to worries and fears about radiation.

We know from epidemiological surveys among atomic-bomb victims in Hiroshima and Nagasaki, if exposure to radiation is greater than 100 millisieverts, 100 mSv, the risk of developing cancer will gradually rise. The risk of developing cancer will not rise, if a person is exposed to less than 100 mSv. Most people measured were exposed to 20 mSv or less.

Note: A 20 mSv exposure for a few days before evacuation, say a week, would result is an exposure of 20/52 = 0.38 mSv/yr which is well within (background + manmade) radiation range.

The Fukushima exposures are below the levels that would cause adverse health effects, taking into account exposure from the atmosphere and ingestion from food.

Regarding the thyroid cancers recently reported in Fukushima: there is no clear link between those cancers and exposure to radiation due to Fukushima, as empirical knowledge shows it takes several years before thyroid cancer is detected after exposure to radiation."

Estimated Future Deaths from Radiation Exposure
According to a recent study, the most likely number of Fukushima cancer deaths will be about 130 OVER THE YEARS; the estimated range is 15 to 1,300

Deaths from Evacuations
After the accident, about 600 deaths occurred due to non-radiological causes, such as mandatory evacuations. Some evacuations were to avoid exposure to radiation, others were due to excessive destruction from the tsunami.

The study estimates evacuations reduced deaths from radiation by 28 OVER THE YEARS; the estimated range is 3 to 245.

Even the "245 lives saved" high-end estimate is less than the deaths due to non-radiological causes.

Deaths from the Tsunami
The above numbers are in addition to the about 20,000 NEAR-INSTANT deaths caused by the tsunami itself. These deaths are not related to nuclear energy generation.

Deaths From Increased Use of Fossil Fuels
After the Fukushima tsunami, Japan idled almost all of its nuclear plants and used energy from fossil fuels to make up for the nuclear energy.

NOTE: With no tsunami anywhere, Germany followed Japan's lead, idled about 50% of its nuclear plants and fired up old coal plants and is building new ones to make up for the nuclear energy.

Nuclear Cybersecurity Facts

The public has been hearing more about the security of nuclear power plant computer systems through fictionalized movies and TV shows, news reports and social media. Here are important facts to know about nuclear plant cyber security.

- The U.S. Nuclear Regulatory Commission (NRC) has extensive regulations in place that are closely monitored and regularly inspected to ensure cyber security at nuclear power plants. The NRC Cyber Security Directorate provides centralized oversight for this important area. This team collaborates with other federal agencies, including the Department of Homeland Security, and other energy regulators and organizations. NRC inspectors are on-site at all U.S. nuclear plants.

- The nuclear energy industry has had a cybersecurity program in place since 2002 to protect critical digital assets and the information they contain from sabotage or malicious use.

- "Critical digital assets" that perform safety, security, and emergency preparedness functions at nuclear power plants are not connected to the Internet.

- Where devices like thumb drives, CDs or laptops are used to interface with plant equipment, strictly monitored measures are in place. Nuclear power plants are well-protected from attacks like Stuxnet, which was transmitted through the use of portable media.

- Nuclear power plants have strong defenses against an insider threat. Individuals who work with digital plant equipment are subject to increased security screening, cyber security training and behavioral observation.

- A cyber attack cannot prevent critical systems in a nuclear energy facility from performing their safety functions. Nuclear power plants are designed to shut down safely if necessary, even if there is a breach of cyber security. They are also designed to automatically disconnect from the power grid if there is a disturbance caused by a cyber attack.

"Nuclear Power Plant Cyber Security: Highly Controlled, Fully Protected," Center for Nuclear Science and Technology Information of the American Nuclear Society.

According to the World Data Bank, Japan's coal generation increased by 57 TWh, natural gas 58 TWh, and oil 9 TWh through 2011. It is reasonable to assume this remained the same through 2012.

Deaths/TWh/yr from coal, gas, oil, and nuclear-based generation are 24, 3, 19.2, and 0.052, respectively. See URL

EXTRA fossil deaths and serious ailments over 2 years:

- Coal = 24 people x 57 TWh x 2 years = 2,736 deaths, plus 25,000 serious ailments

- Gas = 3 x 58 x 2 = 348 deaths, plus 3,400 serious ailments

- Oil = 19.2 x 9 x 2 = 342 deaths, plus 2,900 serious ailments

- Total EXTRA fossil deaths = 2,736 + 348 + 342 = 3,426, plus 31,300 serious ailments

Nuclear = 0.052 x (57 + 58 + 9) x 2 = 13 deaths, plus 54 serious ailments

Opponents of nuclear energy are completely irrational regarding the "dangers of nuclear". Note that natural gas is 8 times less deadly than coal. These deathrates are operative as long as Japan's nuclear plants are idled!!

Fukushima Compared with Other Causes of Death

Deaths from Nuclear vs Coal Energy: If Japan h1ad never adopted nuclear energy generation, accidents and pollution from increased use of coal and gas energy generation would have caused deaths many times greater than those caused by accidents and radiation from nuclear energy generation. Example:

Assuming Japanese nuclear energy production at an average of 250 TWh/yr, annual deaths from nuclear energy generation would be 0.04/(TWh/yr) x 250 TWh/yr = 10, whereas annual deaths from an equal quantity of coal energy generation would be about 50/(TWh/yr) x 250 TWh/yr = 12,500. See below section "DEATHS BY ENERGY SOURCE"

In China, the annual deaths per TWh of coal energy generation is much greater than in Japan. In the US, the annual deaths from coal energy generation is about 15/(TWh/yr) x 1,700 TWh/yr = 25,500; the same order of magnitude as US annual traffic deaths of 34,000.

Note: Deaths from PV solar-rooftop and IWT energy generation are about 16 and 4 times the deaths of nuclear energy generation, respectively, according to the World Health Organization.

Deaths from Cigarettes

Cigarette smoking causes about 1 of every 5 deaths in the United States each year. Cigarette smoking is estimated to cause the following annual deaths:

US: 443,595 deaths per year, of which 49,400 from secondhand smoke exposure; 269,655 among men; 173,940 among women.

Worldwide: Tobacco use causes more than 5 million deaths per year, and current trends show that tobacco use will cause more than 8 million deaths annually by 2030.

http://www.thinkquit.com.au/world_wide_smoking_statistics.shtml

Deaths from Traffic and Cancer: World traffic deaths are about 1.23 million per year, and world cancer deaths are about 8-9 million per year; 7.9 million in 2007.

Background, Manmade and Occupational Radiation Exposure

Background radiation comes from outer space (cosmic, solar), the earth (radon, potassium, uranium, thorium), food, and even other people. US natural background radiation exposure is an average of 3.6 mSv/yr; Australia 2.4 mSv/yr; Ramsar (Iran) 260 mSv/yr

Manmade average exposure is 2.6 mSv/yr, of which CT scans 55%, other diagnostic & therapeutic 24%, other 21% US total radiation exposure (background + manmade) is an average of 3.6 + 2.6 = 6.2 mSv/yr per person, increased from 3.6 mSv/yr about 20 years ago when CT scans were much less common.

The 6.2 mSv/yr average is misleading, because the majority of people have only x-rays during their lifetime, whereas a small percentage of people have CT scans, cancer treatments with radioactive isotopes, angiograms, stent implants, etc. These people have exposures several times greater than 6.2 mSv/yr during their treatment periods.

Example: On October 1, 2011, radiation at a hospital entrance (people walking in and out) near Fukushima in Japan was measured at 0.51 microSv/hr. Someone working at the entrance would be exposed to 0.51 x 2,000 hr/yr = 1.02 mSv/yr which is well within (background + manmade) radiation range. This radiation exposure has to be typed, converted to dose and adjusted with factors to estimate any health impact.

http://theenergycollective.com/willem-post/53939/radiation-exposure

Notable Radiation Events
According to UN and US National Academy of Sciences Reports:

- More than 500 atmospheric atomic device detonations released about 70 billion curies; almost all of it is from instantaneous, short-life, gammy radiation, little from medium and long-life isotopes.

- Chernobyl, 1986, released about 100 million curies; most of it spread as medium and long-life isotopes over a large geographical area; the plant had no concrete containment vessel, as many other former USSR plants.

- Radioactive iodine concentrates in the thyroid which may cause thyroid cancer 2-3 years after exposure. Of all the children exposed by drinking milk from 1986 to 2002, 16 years, about 4,000 were diagnosed with thyroid cancer. As of September 2005, 15 had died, with more to come in future years.

- Fukushima Daiichi, 2011, released about 10 million curies; most of it spread as medium and long-life isotopes by the prevailing winds over the Pacific Ocean.

- Three Mile Island, 1979, released about 50 curies; the plant has a concrete containment vessel, as do all other US nuclear power plants.

Note: Worldwide, nuclear plants without proper containment vessels should be decommissioned and dismantled, i.e., no more Chernobyls!

1 curie = 37 billion atomic disintegrations per second = 37 billion Becqerel

High Radiation Exposure Occupations
Examples of industries with significant occupational radiation exposure IN ADDITION to the above background + manmade exposure:

- Airline crew (the most exposed population), 4.6 mSv/yr

- Industrial radiography

- Medical radiology and nuclear medicine

- Uranium mining

- Nuclear power plant and nuclear fuel reprocessing plant workers, 3.6 mSv/yr

- Research laboratories (government, university and private)

Note: Pilots are more likely to get colon, rectal, prostate and brain cancers; female crew members are twice as likely to suffer breast cancer, and, if pregnant, increase the risk of Down's syndrome and leukemia for their unborn children; the fetus statutory limit is an additional 1 mSv/yr. An explanation for the pilots may be their sedentary working conditions, the poor airline food, the radio headset and the instrument and radar radiation in the cockpit.

Deaths by Energy Source

Much is written about the dangers of nuclear energy. However, it is the safest source of energy for producing electric power, in accordance with studies by the World Health Organization and the european study EXTERNE based on data from past decades. Any deaths due to future global warming, partially the result of the CO_2 from fossil fuels, was not considered by these studies.

The USA: 30,000 deaths/yr from coal pollution of 2,000 TWh/yr, or 15 deaths/yr/TWh, a ratio that will likely remain about the same over the years.

China: 500,000 deaths/yr from coal pollution of 1,800 TWh/yr, or 278 deaths/yr/TWh, a ratio that will likely decline, as China implements safer mining practices and more efficient, cleaner-burning coal power plants over the years.

Energy Source Mortality Rates; Deaths/yr/TWh

- Coal—world average, 161
- Coal—China, 278
- Coal—USA, 15
- Oil—36
- Natural Gas—4
- Biofuel/Biomass—12
- Peat—12
- Solar/rooftop—0.44-0.83
- Wind—0.15
- Hydro—world, 0.10
- Hydro—world*, 1.4
- Nuclear—0.04

* Includes the 170,000 deaths from the failure of the Banquao Reservoir Dam in China in 1975

Studies Underestimate the Risks of Nuclear Power

Jan Beránek

In the following viewpoint, Jan Beránek argues that nuclear power is less safe than several studies of fatalities per gigawatt-year suggest. The Organization for Economic Co-operation and Development (OECD) cites a few studies backing this conclusion. However, all of these studies can be traced to a single collective of Swiss scientists, which to some degree mitigates their scientific value. In addition, these studies exclude deaths from Chernobyl, and rely on probabilistic safety analysis (PSA) rather than field data. Both choices make nuclear power appear safer than it truly is. Once corrected for these irregularities, nuclear power fatalities are far more comparable to fossil fuels. Beránek is the leader of Greenpeace International's Energy Campaign.

As you read, consider the following questions:

1. Why does the author find fault with the Organization for Economic Co-operation and Development (OECD) study?
2. What is the "double standard" the author identifies in plotting nuclear power data?
3. Does the article suggest that fatalities should be the main metric for evaluating energy sources?

"Deaths and energy technologies," by Jan Beránek, Greenpeace International, April 15, 2011. Reprinted by permission. ©Jan Beránek Article.

I n the debate about nuclear power, some people argue that the number of fatalities that can be attributed to the coal or gas industry is much higher than fatalities caused by nuclear power —and conclude that this argument successfully makes the case for the continued use of nuclear reactors.

I find the discussion about which of the dirty technologies (as we actually can and need to get rid of both fossil and nuclear) is largest killer quite indecent and do not want to fuel it by throwing in more abstract figures that never respect the human lives behind them. But for the purpose of getting some clarity around this argument, let's look closer at those claims.

The perhaps most authoritative comparison of fatalities appeared in a number of Organisation for Economic Co-operation and Development (OECD) papers during last decade: "Environmental and Health Impacts of Electricity Generation" published by International Energy Agency in 2002, "Risks and Benefits of Nuclear Energy" published by Nuclear Energy Agency in 2007, "Comparing Nuclear Accident Risks with Those from Other Energy Sources", also published by Nuclear Energy Agency 2010, and "Energy Technology Perspectives 2008" by International Energy Agency. The arguments on fatalities from those papers have been frequently quoted elsewhere.

The first major problem with the fatalities argument that if one takes the effort to look closely, all the relevant figures and graphs in the OECD publications actually refer down to one single collective of authors, which is the Paul Scherer Institute in Switzerland. In references you will find Paul Scherer himself, or his colleagues R. Dones, U. Gantner or S. Hirschberg. Now, having such an important argument based on one single source is not exactly scientific, is it?

Let's look further. Here one fancy version of their graphs, the one that has been reproduced in most influential International Energy Agency (IEA) paper, "Energy Technology Perspectives 2008":

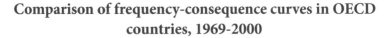

Comparison of frequency-consequence curves in OECD countries, 1969-2000

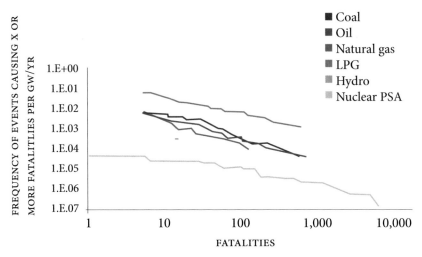

This chart plots frequency of accidents and their fatalities. Therefore, the closer to the left bottom corner the technology appears, the safer it is—and vice versa, the more towards top right corner, the more risky.

You need to note two things that are apparently wrong with this chart. First, it talks about the OECD—which allows authors to entirely exclude the worst nuclear accident—Chernobyl in 1986 - from the picture. If we were to plot Chernobyl, it would appear at the frequency of once in 8,000 GWy (accumulated nuclear generation history by now), and fatalities in the range between 9,000 (according to World Health Report (WHO) report in 2006, future victims in Russia, Byelorussia and Ukraine) and 33,000 (modest estimate of overall potential death toll based on collective dose, see for example TORCH report from 2006). The graph would then actually look like this, with the red bar showing more realistic range for nuclear power's record, making it clearly the most hazardous technology:

The second thing that is terribly wrong with the original chart, is that while it pretends to include nuclear power, it is using double standards to plot it. Contrary to other technologies, where the risks

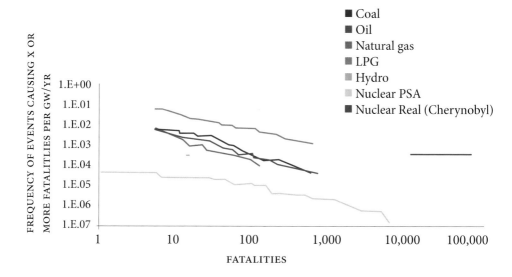

are taken from real world experience, nuclear risks are based on PSA. This is so-called Probabilistic Safety Analysis and is nothing more than a theoretical modeling of reactor risks.

It is acknowledged as a method to identify weak points in the technology, but even the nuclear industry says it is not good tool for coming up with reliable figure of the overall chance of heavy reactor accident. We have seen this method going totally wrong in the case of the US Space Shuttle program, where the engineers estimated a chance of accident as 1 in 100,000 but in fact two of the four Shuttles in the fleet ended up meeting disaster (a great insight by Richard Feynmann can be found here).

We can also see how wrong this method went for the nuclear power sector globally: while the industry is assuring us that the chance of a heavy accident involving reactor damage is in the order of 1 in 100,000 years, in fact we have seen at least five such accidents (one reactor at Three Mile Island in 1979, one reactor at Chernobyl in 1986, and three reactors at Fukushima in 2011) during an accumulated 14,000 reactor-years of experience—this brings the empirical figure of more than 1 in 3,000 chance. Nevertheless, OECD publications use this theoretical calculation, done for a single Swiss reactor (sic!), to make generic conclusions on hazards. This is already a third major methodological mistake that makes the original IEA charts figures heavily biased and unreliable.

So the recipe for cooking up false conclusions about nuclear safety is as easy as this:

1) Take your data from one single institute in all publications (there is a lot of referring in circles but finally it all ends up with the Paul Scherer Institute);

2) Ensure sure you find a methodology that allows you to exclude the worst nuclear disaster in the history from your statistics (such as talking about OECD only); and

3) Use double standards in comparing technologies (theoretical modeling for nuclear versus historical record for other technologies).

While if plotted properly, you will find out that nuclear energy probably still presents the largest risk to lives of the known energy technologies. But there is also an important qualitative difference here. If we talk about accidents in the coal or oil industries, those risking their lives are mostly workers directly involved in the operation. In that sense, it is certainly their choice by choosing the job and they also have the means to mitigate and control the risks they are taking. In the case of nuclear power, most of the risk is imposed on a population that has no information, no expertise, no training, and most importantly no choice as they are denied from having the power to decide if they want a nuclear reactor in their vicinity.

Apart from the International Energy Agency, more graphs and figures have been appearing widely, such as this one

This is coming from yet another angle, which is not only looking at fatalities from accidents but also the health impacts of routine air pollution etc. That this approach gives even much more space for voluntary speculation, it can be illustrated by how much the figures differ if they come from different sources.

Death Rate Per Watts Produced

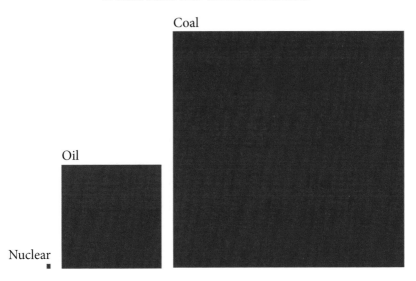

Coal

Oil

Nuclear

Take for example the above mentioned blog and source data for those impressive boxes: they attribute 161 fatalities per one TWh (billion kilowatt hours) of electricity to coal, 36 fatalities per 1 TWh to oil, 4 fatalities per TWh for natural gas, and 0.04 fatalities per TWh to nuclear. That would indicate that nuclear is at least by three magnitudes (1,000 times) safer than fossil fuels.

Contrary to that, New Scientist comes up with figures that still suggest fossil fuels are bigger killers, but the contrast with nuclear is by far less impressive. It concludes that per 1 TWh of generated electricity, there is between 0.02 to 0.12 fatalities attributable to nuclear, 0.03 to 0.16 to gas, and 0.28 to 3.3 to coal. That is roughly a difference of just one magnitude (10-30 times) between nuclear and coal, and nuclear is just comparable to gas.

The nuclear figures seem to be in line with what the International Energy Agency reported in 2002, that is, routine nuclear power related fatalities to be in the range of 0.03 and 0.16 fatalities per TWh only due to health impacts related to uranium mining—even if we simply forget about reactor accidents including Chernobyl.

So the more proper illustration comparing health and death impacts of energy sources—that is if we skip accidents such as

Chernobyl and only talk about standard operation—would rather look like this (grey and black squares representing the range):

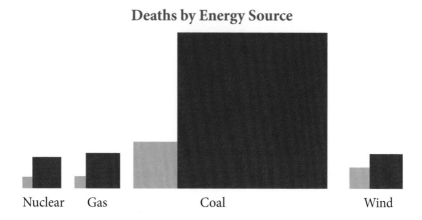

Deaths by Energy Source

Nuclear   Gas   Coal   Wind

And yes, there is no doubt that for various reasons – including the related fatalities but much beyond—we need to get rid of dirty and risky energy sources, be it coal, oil, nuclear, or even gas. The future is with renewable energy technologies which have economic, safety, security of supply, as well as sustainability advantages over fossil and nuclear energy. The fatalities ratio is no differently in clear favour of renewables.

The wind power fatalities per unit of energy was reported to be twice as that of nuclear in Germany in 2000 (IEA 2002). In this chart above, we use the figure of 0.15 per TWh copied from the Next Big Future blog. It is probably safe to assume that in past decade, due to significant upscaling of energy output per one wind turbine, as well as maturing of the technology, the fatality ratio has substantially further decreased.

GLOBAL VIEWPOINTS

CHAPTER 4

Is Nuclear Power a Viable Option for the Future?

Nuclear and Renewable Energy Provide Clean Electricity

Environmental and Energy Study Institute

In the following viewpoint, the relative merits of several energy sources are considered. These break down into a few broad categories. Fossil fuels such as oil, coal, and natural gas are by far the most prevalent energy sources, but they are finite. Moreover, as most of us are aware, fossil fuel use drives climate change because of the greenhouse gases emitted when they are burned. Nuclear energy does not emit carbon, but has economic and safety drawbacks. Despite some reliability issues, renewable energy such as solar and wind are safe, low carbon power sources we should invest in. Finally, conservation and increased efficiency are important components of a sustainable energy future. The Environmental and Energy Study Institute is a nonprofit organization dedicated to promoting environmentally sustainable societies.

As you read, consider the following questions:

1. What is "clean coal," and why are some people skeptical about it?
2. Why isn't natural gas a better solution to low carbon energy?
3. How does nuclear energy compare to cleaner-burning fossil fuels such as natural gas?

F ossil fuels, including coal, oil and natural gas, are currently the world's primary energy source. Formed from organic material over the course of millions of years, fossil fuels have fueled U.S. and global economic development over the past century. Yet fossil fuels are finite resources and they can also irreparably harm the environment. According to the Environmental Protection Agency, the burning of fossil fuels was responsible for 79 percent of U.S. greenhouse gas emissions in 2010. These gases insulate the planet, and could lead to potentially catastrophic changes in the earth's climate. Technologies such as Carbon Capture and Storage (CCS) may help reduce the greenhouse gas emissions generated by fossil fuels, and nuclear energy can be a zero-carbon alternative for electricity generation. But other, more sustainable solutions exist: energy efficiency and renewable energy.

Oil

Oil is the world's primary fuel source for transportation. Most oil is pumped out of underground reservoirs, but it can also be found imbedded in shale and tar sands. Once extracted, crude oil is processed in oil refineries to create fuel oil, gasoline, liquefied petroleum gas, and other nonfuel products such as pesticides, fertilizers, pharmaceuticals, and plastics.

The United States leads the world in petroleum consumption at 19.05 million barrels per day as of 2014. Net petroleum imports for the U.S. were 4.5 million barrels per day. Top exporters to the United States include Canada, Mexico, Saudi Arabia, Venezuela, and Nigeria. Oil poses major environmental problems, and the world's heavy reliance on it for transportation makes it difficult to reduce consumption. Besides the environmental degradation caused by oil spills and extraction, combustion of oil releases fine particulates which can lead to serious respiratory problems, and is a major source of greenhouse gas emissions. Indeed, petroleum is responsible for 42 percent of greenhouse gas emissions in the United States.

Heavier crude oils, especially those extracted from tar sands and shale, require the use of energy intensive methods that result in more emissions and environmental degradation compared to conventional oil. As conventional oil from underground reservoirs runs out, more oil producers are turning to unconventional sources such as tar sands and oil shale.

Coal

Coal is primarily used to generate electricity and is responsible for 39 percent of the electric power supply in the United States in 2014 (down from half in 2007). The United States produces around 11.5 percent of the world's total with Wyoming, West Virginia, Kentucky, Pennsylvania, and Texas leading in production. China is the global leader in coal production, responsible for 45 percent of world supply.

The combustion of coal releases air pollutants such as acid rain-inducing sulfur dioxide, nitrogen oxides (NOx), and mercury. The mining process can also be very damaging to the environment, often resulting in the destruction of vegetation and top-soil. Rivers and streams can also be destroyed or contaminated by mine wastes. The combustion of coal is responsible for 32 percent of the greenhouse gas emissions in the United States.

The premise of "clean coal" has recently been promoted as a way to use this abundant energy source without damaging the environment. Carbon capture and storage (CCS), where carbon is separated from coal and injected underground for long term storage, could theoretically be used to mitigate the coal industry's greenhouse gas emissions. However, CCS has yet to be proven as a safe or realistic way to reduce greenhouse gas emissions from commercial power plants and the environmental and health costs of mining remain.

Natural Gas

Natural gas comprised 27 percent of U.S. energy use in 2014 and is most commonly used to produce heat or electricity for buildings or industrial processes. Less than two percent of U.S. natural gas is used as a transportation fuel, typically for bus fleets. Natural gas is also used to produce fertilizer, paints, and plastics. The United States produces around 19.8 percent of the world's natural gas and consumes about 21.5 percent. Natural gas is most commonly transported by pipeline, which makes Canada the key exporter to the United States, while Russia remains the main supplier for much of Europe. Increasingly, however, natural gas is being transported by ship in a liquefied form (LNG) to meet greater global demand for the fuel.

Natural gas burns cleaner than coal and oil, with almost zero sulfur dioxide emissions and far fewer nitrogen oxide and particulate emissions. Natural gas releases almost 30 percent less carbon dioxide than oil and 43 percent less than coal. However, natural gas is still responsible for 27 percent of greenhouse gas emissions in the United States.

Natural gas, which is primarily composed of methane (CH_4), is also generated by the decomposition of municipal waste in landfills and manure from livestock production. Methane is a greenhouse gas that is more than 20 times as potent as carbon dioxide. Capturing and burning the gas to produce usable heat and power prevents the methane from being released from the landfill or feedlot into the atmosphere directly.

Fossil Fuel Alternatives: Energy Efficiency and Renewable Energy

Despite current U.S. dependence on fossil fuels, several options exist to begin the necessary transition away from a harmful fossil fuel economy. Improving the energy efficiency of buildings, vehicles, industrial processes, appliances and equipment is the most immediate and cost effective way to reduce energy use. Planning communities where people can safely and conveniently use public transit, walk, or bike, instead of using private vehicles, also reduces energy demand. Finally, there are several alternative resources that can supply clean, renewable energy to replace fossil fuels, including water, biomass, wind, geothermal, and solar energy.

In Malaysia, a Warning About the Many Disadvantages Nuclear Power Has

Ronald McCoy

In the following viewpoint, Ronald McCoy identifies several reasons why nuclear power is not an ideal solution to present and future energy needs. First, nuclear power is not cheap. Costs associated with nuclear power, such as insurance and waste disposal, often are obscured by a lack of transparency in accounting. The industry is also in decline, with fifty fewer operational facilities than 2002. Accidents such as at nuclear power plants in Chernobyl and Fukushima and long-term waste management issues provide further disincentives for using nuclear power. The author believes these questions need honest consideration before commitments for new nuclear power projects in Asian nations such as Malaysia can be pursued. McCoy is a retired obstetrician who has served as president of the Malaysian Medical Association, the International Physicians for the Prevention of Nuclear War, and Malaysian Physicians for Social Responsibility.

"Nuclear energy is not a viable option," by Ronald McCoy, published by Consumers Association of Penang, Malaysia. Reprinted by permission.

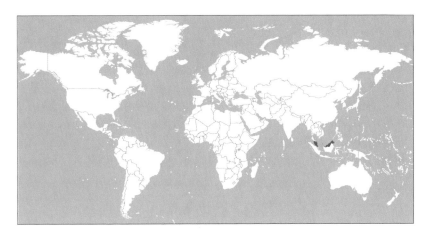

As you read, consider the following questions:

1. Why are the costs of nuclear projects often higher than reported, according to the author?
2. What other economic problems are associated with nuclear energy?
3. Why are officials pushing for nuclear power in Malaysia, and what questions does the author think need to be addressed prior to moving forward?

A speech last week by Dato' Mah Siew Keong, Minister in the Prime Minister's Department, at an event organised by the Asian Strategy and Leadership Institute (ASLI) was reported in Malaysiakini. The minister urged critics of nuclear energy to keep an "open mind," as the government had decided to table the Atomic Energy Regulatory Bill in parliament later this year.

According to the Oxford Advanced Learner's Dictionary, to be open-minded is to be willing to listen to, think about or accept different ideas. It is the opposite of narrow-minded which is to be unwilling to listen to new ideas or to the opinions of others.

The report left me open-mouthed. The dictionary defines "open-mouthed" as having your mouth open because you are surprised or shocked. When I got to the part where the minister claimed that the nuclear debate revolves around three groups -

those who are vocally for it, those who know absolutely nothing about it or those who believe in it as long as it is not in their backyard—my mouth opened wider, the same way it does when I cringe in the dentist's chair.

Perhaps it slipped the minister's mind that there is a fourth group who have carefully thought about nuclear issues over a long period, thoroughly researched the subject of nuclear energy—its economics and finances, its hazards and disasters, its false promises and untested premises, its misinformation and mythology—and have come to the rational conclusion that nuclear energy is not cheap, clean or safe and therefore not an option for any country, particularly a country with democratic deficits, a fettered judicial system, a suppressed media, and disreputable regulatory and law enforcement agencies.

Nuclear energy carries inherent health, security and environmental risks. It is not known to be reliable, affordable, viable, socially acceptable or environmentally sound. The global consensus is that nuclear energy has failed the "market test." Forbes magazine has called it "the biggest managerial disaster in history." Amory Lovins, an energy expert, has called it "the greatest failure of any enterprise in the industrial history of the world," with a litany of financial disasters, including a loss of more than US$1 trillion in subsidies, abandoned projects and other public misadventures.

Nuclear economics

For the sake of open-mindedness and respect for the customary dental stance, I would strongly urge the minister and his cohorts in Malaysia, the Malaysia Nuclear Power Corporation, to study the recently published World Nuclear Industry Status Report 2014 (WNISR 2014). In 139 pages, it analyses the rapid changes in nuclear economics, the technology revolution in the power sector, and the impact of renewable energy on the financial viability and status of nuclear power. The report predicts that the use of renewable energy will increase rapidly, that investment in renewable energy sources will be dominant, and that investment in solar and wind power will exceed investment in fossil fuels or nuclear power.

Cheap nuclear energy is a myth. Misleading claims that it is cheap are often based on unverifiable bottom-line results or 'justified' by analyses with hidden assumptions that are highly favourable to the nuclear industry. The total economic cost of nuclear energy is difficult to determine, as the industry's accounting methods lack transparency. Costs for accident insurance, waste disposal and decommissioning are often buried in enormously generous government subsidies or conjured into debt legacies for future generations.

The nuclear industry is in decline worldwide. Today only 31 countries are operating a total of 388 nuclear reactors, compared with 438 in 2002. Several nuclear reactor projects have been indefinitely delayed or cancelled. The share of nuclear power in the world's power production has declined from 17.6 per cent in 1996 to 10.8 per cent in 2013.

Only 14 countries have plans to build new reactors. Sixty-seven reactors are currently classified as "under construction." Forty-nine of them have met with significant delays, ranging from several months to several years. Eight of them have been "under construction" for more than 20 years, including one in the United States which began in 1972. France, Finland and China are working on "next generation" reactors which they claim have "higher efficiency and advanced safety systems," but they are bogged down in delays and cost overruns.

The cost of constructing a reactor largely determines the final cost of nuclear electricity, particularly when numerous construction delays and cost overruns impact budgets significantly. Estimates of investment costs have risen in the past decade from US$1,000 to around US$8,000 per installed kilowatt.

According to the French Court of Accounts, the cost of generating nuclear power increased by 21 per cent between 2010 and 2013. Germany, Sweden and the United States are closing down reactors because projected income does not cover operating costs. Debt levels remain very high amongst European nuclear power companies. The two largest French groups (EDF and GDF-Suez) and the two largest German utilities (E.ON and RWE) equally share a total of more than US$173 billion in debt. Since 2008, Europe's top ten utilities have lost half of their US$1.4 trillion share value.

There is conclusive evidence that electricity generated from nuclear power is far more costly than electricity from fossil fuels or renewables. The ratings and risk firm, Moody's Corporate Finances, recently estimated that nuclear energy's capital cost per kilowatt was 275 per cent higher than that of wind energy and 150 per cent higher than solar energy. It predicts that nuclear costs will rise further, while the cost of renewable energy sources will be substantially reduced.

Fukushima

Accidents are inevitable in nuclear power plants. Between 1952 and 2009, there were 99 minor nuclear accidents worldwide, each with the potential to develop into a major disaster. Major nuclear reactor accidents are not common, but when they do occur they can be catastrophic, as in Chernobyl and Fukushima.

The meltdown of three nuclear reactors in Fukushima in March 2011 has brought Japan to its knees, reinforced worldwide fears of nuclear accidents, and highlighted the nuclear industry's failure to prevent accidents and near misses. A Greenpeace report, Lessons from Fukushima, has revealed that the Fukushima accident was caused mainly by the institutional failures of the Japanese nuclear industry, its regulators and the Japanese government. There was failure to acknowledge and anticipate nuclear risks and to enforce appropriate nuclear safety standards. After the accident, there was failure to protect the public in a dire emergency situation and later to provide appropriate compensation for the victims.

Since the disaster three years ago, serious challenges remain. Radiation readings inside the buildings continue to make direct human intervention almost impossible. Massive amounts of water, about 360 tons per day, are still being pumped into the destroyed reactors to cool fuel rods. This constantly increasing volume of contaminated radioactive water is stored in tanks which have started to leak. Experts say that the Japanese government will soon be left with no choice but to release radioactive water into the ocean.

Thousands of Japanese are still exposed to radiation, while the Japanese government and the Tokyo Electric Power Company flounder in their efforts to contain the disaster. Their daily lives have been disrupted and they have lost their homes, their jobs, their businesses, their farms, their communities, and their way of life. More than 130,000 people in Fukushima have been evacuated. and another 137,000 people are living in temporary housing. About 1,700 deaths have been officially recorded.

The truth is that no one in the world really knows how to deal with the Fukushima accident. It is a wake-up call for all thirty countries operating nuclear power plants and for those governments still planning to build nuclear reactors, such as Malaysia with its defective safety and maintenance culture and unreliable regulatory attitudes. Chernobyl and Fukushima have made it clear that there is no such thing as nuclear safety or a fail-safe nuclear reactor. Human error and unpredictable events are unavoidable. Murphy's Law is inexorable: If anything can go wrong, in time it will go wrong. A major nuclear accident in Malaysia could render large areas of land uninhabitable for thousands of years.

Interminable radioactive nuclear waste

Nuclear waste remains radioactive for thousands of years, making nuclear power inherently and irredeemably hazardous. There is still absolutely no way to safely and permanently dispose of the waste. This is the most dangerous and unacceptable feature of nuclear power plants. In other words, the promotion of nuclear energy by the Malaysian government is tantamount to the promotion of interminable, lethal, radioactive nuclear waste.

The nuclear industry's so-called solutions to radioactive waste only exist in theory, such as the theoretical Generation IV Integral Fast Reactor for reprocessing spent nuclear fuel or alternatively the burying of nuclear waste in deep geological repositories. None of these so-called "solutions" exists anywhere in the world. Nuclear power plants continue to store their radioactive waste temporarily under water in pools, located alongside reactors.

For example, plutonium has a half-life of 24,400 years. In other words, it will take 24,400 years (or 244 centuries) for the radioactivity of any given quantity of plutonium to be reduced by half. And it will take another 24,400 years for the remaining radioactivity in the plutonium to be reduced by another half. In practical terms, there will be no end to its radioactivity.

If medieval man had resorted to nuclear power, we in the 21st century today would still be burdened with the management of his waste, assuming it had not terminated life on the planet. If the Malaysian government opts for nuclear energy, it will knowingly bequeath unmanageable lethal nuclear waste to future generations. If we don't stop this move, we will all be guilty of premeditated genocide, especially when there is an alternative sustainable energy source—renewable energy.

Renewable energy

In 2013, renewable energy emerged as a safe, flexible, easily deployed energy source, with a lower carbon footprint than nuclear power. Many governments have recognised that fact and have sensibly started to develop and rely on renewable energy.

Spain has generated more power from wind than any other source—wind power represents 21 per cent of total power and exceeds nuclear power. It is the first time that wind has become the largest electricity source over an entire year in any country. Excluding large hydro-power, Spain, Brazil, China, Germany, India and Japan produce more power from renewables than from nuclear power.

The International Panel on Climate Change (IPCC) suggests that reducing carbon emissions will require a reduction in the use of fossil fuels and an increase in low-carbon energy sources. Renewable energy accounted for just over half of the new electricity-generating capacity added globally in 2012, led by growth in wind, hydro and solar power. The IPCC envisages the gradual phase-out of nuclear power, within the framework of meeting carbon emissions reduction targets.

Global investment in renewable energy—excluding large hydro—amounted to US$214 billion in 2013, four times the 2004 total of US$52 billion. Since 2000, there has been a 25 per cent annual growth rate for wind and 43 per cent for solar PV, while nuclear power declined by 0.4 per cent.

Variable renewable energy sources (VRE), like solar and wind, are weather dependent and not fully predictable. By predicting ahead, traditional base load is likely to disappear completely in several countries at certain times of the year. The concept of a centralised base-load capacity is being reexamined in many countries with the likelihood that it will be replaced with a new, flexible, decentralised energy system, with smart distributed grids, renewable energy sources, and high levels of efficiency. There is no place for nuclear energy in such a new system.

Conclusion

In June 2009, the Malaysian government singled out nuclear energy as one of the options for electricity generation, in order to reduce carbon emissions from fossil fuels, to meet future energy demands, and achieve energy diversification. A year later, the deployment of nuclear energy was identified as one of the Entry Point Projects in the Economic Transformation Programme and the Malaysia Nuclear Power Corporation (MNPC) was assigned the role of spearheading, planning and coordinating the implementation of a nuclear energy development programme that is expected to culminate in the delivery of Malaysia's first nuclear power plant by 2021.

The MNPC argues that nuclear energy is a valid energy option, if there are suitable sites for nuclear power plants, strong community support, and international safeguards applied by the International Atomic Energy Agency (IAEA), which promotes the peaceful uses of nuclear energy but is seen to be a creature of the nuclear industry, with obvious conflicts of interest.

There is a lot of disinformation about the virtues of nuclear energy and the Malaysian government and nuclear proponents need to answer some serious questions. Where is the strong community support in the country for nuclear energy? Where is the process of genuine dialogue, debate and consultation with the people of Malaysia? Where is the evidence that nuclear energy is cheap, clean and safe? What is the real cost of nuclear energy? What about the enormous subsidies required? How concerned are you about the serious health and environmental dangers of nuclear energy? And most critically, how are you going to manage the safe disposal of lethal nuclear waste which will remain radioactive for thousands of years? Do you not have a moral responsibility for the safety and welfare of future generations?

There are times in the history of a country when critically important decisions must be made correctly and democratically, with considerable care, honesty, and wisdom, because such decisions will have a lasting and crucial impact on the country's future. Whether or not to opt for nuclear power is such a decision. In determining Malaysia's portfolio of energy resources, we must isolate and quarantine the issue of nuclear energy from politics, cronyism, personal gain, duplicity and foolishness.

Most governments in the world have seen the writing on the nuclear wall and are phasing out nuclear energy and investing in renewable energy, energy efficiency technologies and energy conservation. The Malaysia government will be seen to be indifferent, if not delinquent, if it ignores sensible global trends and proceeds to build a nuclear power plant, which could be potentially catastrophic, nation-crippling, and a radioactive time bomb for future generations.

Today's Nuclear Plants Are Safer than Before, Thanks to Disasters in Ukraine and the United States

Jack Spencer and Nicolas Loris

In the following viewpoint, Jack Spencer and Nicolas Loris assert that close calls and accidents have led to increased nuclear power safety measures. In 1979, a meltdown nearly occurred at the Three Mile Island nuclear power plant in Pennsylvania. The operators misjudged a cooling circuit pump failure, causing a discharge of radioactive steam. Luckily, the levels of radioactivity were very low and did not harm humans or animals in the vicinity. The plant received several safety upgrades including fire protection and enhanced emergency preparedness. The most destructive nuclear accident in history, Chernobyl, resulted from operator error and design flaws. It is unlikely to happen in modern plants. Spencer is a research fellow in nuclear energy. Loris is a research assistant in the Thomas A. Roe Institute for Economic Policy Studies at The Heritage Foundation.

As you read, consider the following questions:

1. What happened at Three Mile Island?
2. How did the Chernobyl meltdown differ from Three Mile Island in cause and effect?
3. What technology improvements followed these accidents?

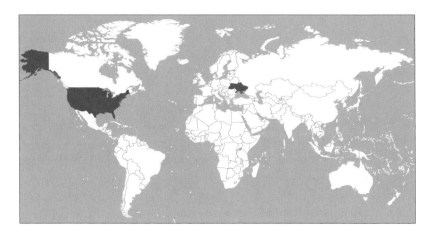

This Saturday marks the 30th anniversary of the partial meltdown of the Three Mile Island (TMI) nuclear reactor. This occasion is a good time to consider the advances in nuclear power safety since that time and discuss the misinformation about this incident and the 1986 nuclear accident in Chernobyl, Ukraine, which is often associated with TMI.

Three Mile Island: What Happened

On March 28, 1979, a cooling circuit pump in the non-nuclear section of Three Mile Island's second station (TMI-2) malfunctioned, causing the reactor's primary coolant to heat and internal pressure to rise. Within seconds, the automated response mechanism thrust control rods into the reactor and shut down the core. An escape valve opened to release pressure but failed to close properly. Control room operators only saw that a "close" command was sent to the relief valve, but nothing displayed the valve's actual position.[1] With the valve open, coolant escaped through the pressurizer, sending misinformation to operators that there was too much pressure in the coolant system. Operators then shut down the water pumps to relieve the "pressure."

Operators allowed coolant levels inside the reactor to fall, leaving the uranium core exposed, dry, and intensely hot. Even though inserting control rods halted the fission process, the

TMI-2 reactor core continued to generate about 160 megawatts of "decay" heat, declining over the next three hours to 20 megawatts. [2] Approximately one-third of the TMI-2 reactor was exposed and began to melt.

By the time operators discovered what was happening, superheated and partially radioactive steam built up in auxiliary tanks, which operators then moved to waste tanks through compressors and pipes. The compressors leaked. The steam leakage released a radiation dose equivalent to that of a chest X-ray scan, about one-third of the radiation humans absorb in one year from naturally occurring background radiation.[3] No damage to any person, animal, or plant was ever found.[4]

The Outcome
The local population of 2 million people received an average estimated dose of about 1 millirem—miniscule compared to the 100-125 millirems that each person receives annually from naturally occurring background radiation in the area. Nationally, the average person receives 360 millirems per year.[5]

No significant radiation effects on humans, animals, or plants were found. In fact, thorough investigation and sample testing of air, water, milk, vegetation, and soil found that there were negligible effects and concluded that the radiation was safely contained.[6] The most recent and comprehensive study was a 13-year evaluation of 32,000 people living in the area that found no adverse health effects or links to cancer.[7]

Technological Improvements and Lessons Learned
A number of technological and procedural changes have been implemented by industry and the Nuclear Regulatory Commission (NRC) to considerably reduce the risk of a meltdown since the 1979 incident. These include:

- Plant design and equipment upgrades, including fire protection, auxiliary feedwater systems, containment building isolation, and automatic plant shut down capabilities;

- Enhanced emergency preparedness, including closer coordination between federal, state, and local agencies;

- Integration of NRC observations, findings, and conclusions about plant performance and management into public reports;

- Regular plant performance analysis by senior NRC managers who identify plants that require additional regulatory attention;

- Expansion of NRC's resident inspector program, whereby at least two inspectors live nearby and work exclusively at each plant;

- Expanded performance- and safety-oriented inspections;

- Additional accident safety equipment to mitigate and monitor conditions during accidents; and[8]

- Establishment of the Institute for Nuclear Power Operators, an industry-created non-profit organization that evaluates plants, promotes training and information sharing, and helps individual plants overcome technical issues.

Chernobyl: What Happened

Seven years after the incident at Three Mile Island, on April 25, 1986, a crew of engineers with little background in reactor physics began an experiment at the Chernobyl nuclear station. They sought to determine how long the plant's turbines' inertia could provide power if the main electrical supply to the station was cut. Operators chose to deactivate automatic shutdown mechanisms to carry out their experiment.[9]

The four Chernobyl reactors were known to become unstable at low power settings,[10] and the engineers' experiment caused the reactors to become exactly that. When the operators cut power and switched to the energy from turbine inertia, the coolant pump system failed, causing heat and extreme steam pressure to build inside the reactor core. The reactor experienced a power surge and exploded, blowing off the cover lid of the reactor building, and spewed radioactive gasses and flames for nine days.

The episode was exacerbated by a second design flaw: The Chernobyl reactors lacked fully enclosed containment buildings, a basic safety installation for commercial reactors in the U.S.[11]

The Outcome
Chernobyl was the result of human error and poor design. Of the approximately 50 fatalities, most were rescue workers who entered contaminated areas without being informed of the danger.

The World Heath Organization says that up to 4,000 fatalities could ultimately result from Chernobyl-related cancers. Though these could still emerge, as yet, they have not. The primary health effect was a spike in thyroid cancer among children, with 4,000-5,000 children diagnosed with the cancer between 1992 and 2002. Of these, 15 children unfortunately died. Though these deaths were unquestionably tragic, no clear evidence indicates any increase in other cancers among the most heavily affected populations.

Interestingly, the World Health Organization has also identified a condition called "paralyzing fatalism," which is caused by "persistent myths and misperceptions about the threat of radiation."[12] In other words, the propagation of ignorance by anti-nuclear activists has caused more harm to the affected populations than has the radioactive fallout from the actual accident. Residents of the area assumed a role of "chronic dependency" and developed an entitlement mentality because of the meltdown.[13]

Technology Improvements and Lessons Learned
Comparing the technology of the nuclear reactor at Chernobyl to U.S. reactors is not fair. First, the graphite-moderated, water-cooled reactor at Chernobyl maintained a high positive void coefficient. While the scientific explanation[14] of this characteristic is not important, its real-life application is. Essentially, it means that under certain conditions, coolant inefficiency can cause heightened reactivity. In other words, its reactivity can rapidly increase as

its coolant heats (or is lost) resulting in more fissions, higher temperatures, and ultimately meltdown.[15]

This is in direct contrast to the light-water reactors used in the United States, which would shut down under such conditions. U.S. reactors use water to both cool and moderate the reactor. The coolant keeps the temperature from rising too much, and the moderator is used to sustain the nuclear reaction. As the nuclear reaction occurs, the water heats up and becomes a less efficient moderator (cool water facilitates fission better than hot water), thus causing the reaction to slow down and the reactor to cool. This characteristic makes light water reactors inherently safe and is why a Chernobyl-like reactor could never be licensed in the U.S.

Given the inherent problems with the Chernobyl reactor design, many technological changes and safety regulations were put in place to prevent another Chernobyl-like meltdown from occurring. Designers renovated the reactor to make it more stable at lower power, have the automatic shutdown operations activate quicker, and have automated and other safety mechanisms installed.[16]

Chernobyl also led to the formation of a number of international efforts to promote nuclear power plant safety through better training, coordination, and implantation of best practices. The World Association of Nuclear Operators is one such organization and includes every entity in the world that operates a nuclear power plant.

Myths Persist

The circumstances, causes, and conditions of the Chernobyl meltdown are far removed from the American experience. Important lessons should be taken from both accidents. Thankfully, many improvements in the technology and regulatory safety of nuclear reactors are among them.

References

[1]World Nuclear Association, "Three Mile Island: 1979," March 2001, at *http://www. world-nuclear.org/info/inf36.html* (March 26, 2009).

[2]Smithsonian Institution, National Museum of American History, "Three Mile Island: The Inside Story," at*http://americanhistory. si.edu/tmi/tmi03.htm* (March 26, 2009).

[3]American Nuclear Society, "What Happened and What Didn't in the TMI-2 Accident," at*http://www.ans.org/pi/resources/sptopics /tmi/whathappened.html* (March 26, 2009).

[4]U.S. Nuclear Regulatory Commission, "Fact Sheet on the Three Mile Island Accident," *http://www.nrc.gov/reading-rm/doc-collections/fact-sheets/3mile-isle. html* (March 26, 2009).

[5]United States Department of Energy, Office of Civilian Radioactive Waste Management, "Facts About Radiation," *OCRWM Fact Sheet*, January 2005, at *http://www. ocrwm.doe.gov/factsheets/doeymp0403.shtml* (November 6, 2008).

[6]Nuclear Regulatory Commission, "Fact Sheet on the Three Mile Island Accident."

[7]World Nuclear Association, "Three Mile Island: 1979."

[8] Fact Sheet on the Three Mile Island Accident" Nuclear Regulatory Commission at *http://www.nrc.gov/reading-rm/doc-collections/fact-sheets/3mile-isle.html* (June 24, 2008).

[9]For full description of what caused the accident at Chernobyl, see Richard Rhodes, *Nuclear Renewal* (New York: Penguin Books, 1993), ch. 5.

[10]World Nuclear Association, "Chernobyl Accident," May 2008, at *http://www.world-nuclear.org/info/chernobyl/inf07.html*(March 26, 2009).

[11]Simon Rippon et al., "The Chernobyl Accident," *Nuclear News*, June 1986, at/static/ reportimages/5484F39EEAE25F81A8685A27103E7A0A.pdf (March 26, 2009).

[12]Press release, "Chernobyl: The True Scale of the Accident," World Health Organization, International Atomic Energy Agency, and U.N. Development Programme, September 5, 2005, at*http://www.who.int/mediacentre/news/releases/2005/pr38/en/print. html* (November 6, 2008).

[13]World Nuclear Association, "Chernobyl Accident."

[14]"Neutron Kinetics of the Chernobyl Accident," *ENS News*, Summer 2006, at *http:// www.euronuclear.org/e-news/e-news-13/neutron-kinetics.htm* (March 27, 2009).

[15]International Atomic Energy Agency, "The Chernobyl Accident: Updating of INSAG-1," 1992, at *http://www-pub.iaea.org/MTCD /publications/PDF/Pub913e_web.pdf* (August 27, 2008).

[16]*Ibid.*

In the United States, Risk Must Be Balanced with Consequences When Considering Nuclear Energy

Gary Was

In the following viewpoint, Gary Was argues that the benefits of nuclear energy are tremendous and should not be ignored simply because of the risks of catastrophe. Was compares the probability of dying in a nuclear disaster to more common causes of death— including deaths from some other energy sources—to put into perspective the risks inherent in using nuclear power. Nuclear power is so heavily regulated in the United States, he argues, that fear should not be a motivator in dismissing it as a potential clean energy source. Was is a professor of nuclear engineering and radiological sciences; material science and engineering; and the Walter J. Weber, Jr. Professor of Sustainable Energy, Environmental and Earth Systems Engineering at the University of Michigan.

As you read, consider the following questions:

1. When did the United States begin operating nuclear plants?
2. Why wouldn't the Chernobyl reactor have been licensed in the United States?
3. How long does unprocessed nuclear waste take to return to benign radiation levels?

Nuclear power is likely the least well-understood energy source in the United States. Just 99 nuclear power plants spread over 30 states provide one-fifth of America's electricity. These plants have provided reliable, affordable and clean energy for decades. They also carry risk—to the public, to the environment and to the financial solvency of utilities.

Risk is the product of the probability of an occurrence and its consequence. The probability of dying in a car accident is actually quite high compared to other daily events, but such accidents usually claim few individuals at a time, and so the risk is low. The reason nuclear energy attracts so much attention is that while the probability of a catastrophic event is extremely low, the consequence is often perceived to be extremely high.

Nuclear power and public risk

In the US, commercial nuclear plants have been operating since the late 1960s. If you add up the plants' years in operation, they average about 30 years each, totaling about 3,000 reactor years of operating experience. There have been no fatalities to any member of the public due to the operation of a commercial nuclear power plant in the US. Our risk in human terms is vanishingly low.

Nuclear power's safety record is laudable, considering that nuclear plants are running full-tilt. The average capacity factor of these plants exceeds 90%; that means 99 plants are generating full power over 90% of the time.

If you compare that to any other energy form, there's a huge gap. Coal is a mainstay of electricity generation in this country and has a capacity factor of around 65%. Gas is about the same; wind's capacity factor is around is 30%, and solar is at 25%.

While the probability of a nuclear catastrophe is extremely low, it is only part of the risk calculation. The other part of risk is consequence. The world has been host to three major nuclear power generation accidents: Three Mile Island in 1979, Chernobyl in 1986 and Fukushima in 2011. To the best of our knowledge, Three Mile Island, while terribly frightening, resulted in no health consequences to the public.

Chernobyl was an unmitigated disaster in which the reactor vessel—the place where the nuclear fuel produces heat—was ruptured and the graphite moderator in the reactor ignited, causing an open-air fire and large releases of radioactive material. This reactor design would never have been licensed to operate in the Western world because it lacked a containment.

The scientific consensus on the effects of the disaster as developed by the United Nations Scientific Committee on the Effects of Atomic Radiation (UNSCEAR) has identified 66 deaths from trauma, acute radiation poisoning and cases of thyroid cancer. Additional deaths may occur over time, as understanding the causes of death is a statistical rather than a deterministic process. Considering that the authorities didn't alert the neighboring communities for many hours, the long-term health consequences of that reactor accident are surprisingly small.

And then there was Fukushima Daiichi. At least three of the reactors have sustained core damage, and there is potentially damage to the reactor vessel as well. At this time, no deaths have been attributed to radiation release at Fukushima, but an estimated 1,600 people died as a result of evacuation, and land contamination was widespread.

So if you look at these cases together, in Chernobyl, you had a reactor core on fire and open to the air; in Fukushima, three reactors lost all power during full operation and sustained major core damage, resulting in substantial radioactivity release in one of the most densely populated countries in the world.

These accidents had serious, lasting consequences that aren't to be trivialized, but the consequences are nothing like what has been feared and glorified in movies over the past 50 years. What we've learned about public risk during that time is that the forecasted nightmares resulting from nuclear accidents, even in serious accidents, simply haven't come to fruition. At the same time, as a society, we've come to accept—or at least look the other way from—thousands of traffic- or coal-related deaths every year in the US alone.

Waste containment: risk and storage

The production of energy in any form alters the environment. Coal and natural gas generate particulates, greenhouse gases and the like. In 2012, coal plants in the US generated 110 million tons of coal ash. Nuclear waste created by power generation is in solid form, and the volume is minuscule in comparison, but extremely toxic. Even the production of wind and solar energy generates waste.

Fuel for nuclear plants is in the form of fuel assemblies or bundles, each containing tubes of a zirconium alloy that hold hundreds of ceramic pellets of uranium oxide.

Each fuel assembly provides power for four to five years before it is removed. After removal, the fuel is considered to be waste and must be safely stored, as its radiotoxicity level is extremely high. Unprocessed, it takes about 300,000 years for the radiation level of the waste inside an assembly to return to background levels, at which point it is benign.

Due to the cancellation of the Yucca Mountain site in Nevada, there is no place designated for long-term nuclear waste storage in the US, and utilities have resorted to constructing on-site storage at their plants. These storage containers were not designed to be permanent, and the Nuclear Regulatory Commission (NRC) is now licensing these temporary facilities for up to 100 years.

Many cheered when the Yucca Mountain project was shuttered, but waste still must be stored, and clearly it is safer to store the waste in a single, permanent depository than in 99 separate and temporary structures.

Monitored, retrievable storage is the safest approach to nuclear waste storage. Waste sites could be centralized and continuously monitored, and built in such a way that waste canisters could be retrieved if, for example, storage technology improves, or if it becomes economical to reprocess the waste to recover the remaining uranium and plutonium created during operation.

If we are to keep using nuclear power even at the present rate, our risks related to waste will increase every year until storage is addressed thoughtfully and thoroughly.

Infrastructure: same plant, different century

At the dawn of commercial nuclear power, the prospect of cheap, plentiful energy produced forecasts that nuclear energy would be too cheap to meter—we'd all be ripping the meters off our houses. But as plant designs evolved, it became clear that ensuring safety would increase the cost of the energy produced.

Every accident taught us something, and with every accident the NRC unveiled a new set of regulations, resulting in a system of plants that are, from the perspective of a few decades ago, much safer. Such tight regulatory oversight, while needed, drives up cost and means that utilities undertake significant financial risk with each nuclear plant they build.

Decades ago, the idea that the NRC would be granting 20-year license extensions to power plants was unheard of. Today, 75% of plants have received them. Now there's talk about a second round of license extensions, and the NRC, the US Department of Energy and the industry are engaged in talking about what it would take to get a third. We're talking about 80 or even 100 years of operation, in which case a plant would outlive the Earth's population at the time it was built.

In the shorter term, life extension makes sense. Most of the plants in the United States are Generation 2 plants, but Generation 3 is being built all over the world. Gen 2 plants are proving very robust, and existing plants are quite economical to operate. Gen 3 plants, like Vogtle now being built in Georgia, boast better safety systems, better structural components and better design.

Would I rather have one of those than the one I have now? Absolutely. The risk of operating such a facility is simply lower. At US$4.5 billion to $10 billion, Gen 3 plants are very expensive to build, but we must either accept that capital outlay or find another source of electricity that has all the benefits of nuclear energy.

How much risk do we accept?

As a society, we accepted over 32,000 traffic accident deaths in 2013, and no one stopped driving as a result.

I think most people would be surprised to know that in 2012, seven million people globally died from health complications due to air pollution and that an estimated 13,000 US deaths were directly attributable to fossil-fired plants.

US deaths from coal represent an annual catastrophe that exceeds that of all nuclear accidents over all time. In fact, nuclear power has prevented an estimated 1.84 million air-pollution related deaths worldwide. Natural gas plants, increasingly being constructed around the country, are highly subject to price volatility and, while cleaner than coal, they still account for 22% of carbon dioxide emissions from electricity generation in the US. This is not to mention the illogical use of this precious resource for electricity generation versus uses for which it is more uniquely suited, such as heating homes or powering vehicles.

And until the capacity factor for renewables increases dramatically, the cost drops and large-scale storage is developed, they are simply not equipped to handle the bulk of US energy needs nor to provide electricity on demand.

Through the NRC's oversight and the work of researchers all over the world, we have applied lessons from every global nuclear event to every American nuclear plant. The risk inherent in nuclear plant operation will always be present, but it is one of the world's most rigorously monitored activities, and its proven performance in delivering zero-carbon electricity is one that shouldn't be dismissed out of fear.

Nuclear Power's Economics and Climate Benefits Do Not Justify Public Health Risks

Peter Karamoskos

In the following excerpted viewpoint, Peter Karamoskos explains the nuclear industry's pattern of rebranding itself to suit current crises. In the oil shocks of the 1970s for example, nuclear power was marketed as the key to energy security. Karamoskos situates the current nuclear "renaissance" spurred on by the hope for a zero carbon energy source to combat climate change in this context. Once again, nuclear energy will not deliver, according to the Karamoskos. In his view, the public health risks and related costs associated with the nuclear fuel cycle should not be eclipsed by the economic and climate-based arguments in its favor. Karamoskos is a nuclear radiologist; the treasurer of the Medical Association for the Prevention of War (MAPW), the treasurer of the International Campaign for the Abolition of Nuclear Weapons (ICAN), and the public representative of the Radiation Health Committee, Australian Radiation Protection and Nuclear Safety Agency (ARPANSA).

"Nuclear power & public health," by Peter Karamoskos, *Evatt Journal*, Vol. 10, No. 1, December 2011, http://evatt.org.au/papers/nuclear-power-public-health.html. Reprinted by permission.

As you read, consider the following questions:

1. How has nuclear power's efforts to distance itself from its military origins as a benevolent and necessary technology changed throughout its history?
2. What is ionoising radiation, and how does it affect public health?
3. Which often ignored or downplayed aspects of the nuclear fuel cycle does the author focus on?

Introduction

The public health implications for a resurgence of nuclear power appear to have taken a subordinate position to the economic and global warming arguments that the industry has advanced to justify its expansion. The purpose of this essay is several-fold: to review the scientific evidence for the public health impacts of nuclear power; to assess occupational hazards faced by workers in the nuclear industry involved in the nuclear fuel cycle; to assess the evidence for nuclear reactor safety and critically challenge the underlying assumptions. This paper will also examine the public health risks of spent fuel from nuclear power reactors. The common thread linking these safety issues is the risk posed to public health by ionising radiation and in particular the risk of cancer. The nuclear industry and our understanding of radioactive health hazards developed in tandem during the 20th century, but the relationship has always been uneasy and often in conflict. A brief historical narrative of this joint evolution is essential to understanding the context and scope of the health issues at the heart of the debate.

If we are to believe the nuclear industry, nuclear power is both safe and vital to our future, yet over half a century of nuclear power has proven both contentions false. In the last decade, the nuclear power industry has undergone a "renaissance" of interest and hype, spurred along by the claim that it is vital to combating global warming. The industry has had many false starts, each time failing to live up to its promises. At its inception, it sold itself as providing limitless electricity too cheap to meter. When this was proven false, it attempted to recreate itself as the key to energy security during the oil shocks of the 1970s. But it foundered again on the grounds that it was not only too expensive and most electricity did not rely on imported oil, it was so economically unattractive that financing was virtually impossible without heavy tax-payer subsidies and loan guarantees. Throughout this period, public health concerns increased against a backdrop of reactor safety concerns and the effects of ionising radiation on the surrounding populations, with ten core meltdowns in various nuclear reactors, including several in nuclear power reactors, culminating in the Chernobyl disaster of 1986.

The link between nuclear power and nuclear weapons is critical in understanding the context of the industry's development and its impact on public health and safety. Nuclear power followed the development of nuclear weapons in the USA in an attempt to garner public support for nuclear technology, which had shown how destructive it could be and how much of a threat it posed to humanity. Public tax-payer support was critical to facilitate further weapons development. Nuclear power was the product of the "Atoms for Peace" program in the 1950s to achieve this end, leading to the export of nuclear reactor technology as well as bomb-grade highly enriched uranium as reactor fuel to many countries. Propelled by the "more is better" hubristic military commanders and civilian nuclear boosters, in attempting to highlight the "peaceful atom," the nuclear establishment inadvertently although not unpredictably led to illicit weapons programs around the world.

The original drivers of nuclear power were not a need for electricity, environmental concerns, or the need for energy security, but the political and military imperatives that dominated and spurred its development. In this climate, safety issues were not paramount. How could they be if the science of the human effects of ionising radiation was still in its infancy and the safety of nuclear reactors unknown? If anything, safety concerns posed potential obstacles to the industry's development and needed to be managed, as they were by savvy media men. It was a climate of "electricity today, and (maybe) safety tomorrow."

The questions are: what is different now? Is nuclear power now safe?

The history of human health and the safety of nuclear power is inexorably intertwined with the evolving history of the health effects of ionising radiation (IR). Whereas the science underpinning the generation of electricity from nuclear power is well established, the health effects on humans of ionising radiation is still evolving. This is not to undermine the voluminous research and findings clearly documenting the adverse effects of ionising radiation on human beings. That much is well documented and understood. The uncertainties lie in precisely quantifying the effects of IR, including defining the risks of ever decreasing doses with greater precision. This is the key in attempting to understand the direct adverse health effects of nuclear power on two groups; nuclear industry workers and populations in the vicinity of nuclear reactors and subject to their radioactive emissions.

Ionising radiation & public health

Ionising radiation arises from many sources. Nuclear fission which powers nuclear reactors is one. It is postulated that ionising radiation imparts its deleterious health effects through two mechanisms: transference of its energy to atoms in biological tissue which then becomes electrically charged, leading to the formation of free radicals that then damage the cell's genetic blueprint (DNA) and lead to genetic mutations; and direct DNA disruption along the track the ionising radiation traverses through the cell's nucleus. The most mutagenic (causing genetic mutations) of these are double stranded breaks (DSB), where both strands of the double helix DNA molecule are simultaneously disrupted and the result is a high likelihood of mutations. This then predisposes to the initiation of cancer when the regulatory mechanisms of the cell fail. Cancer may not appear for 10–40 years (latency), although the time can be as short as five years for leukaemia. Ionising radiation is classified as a Class 1 carcinogen by the International Agency for Research in Cancer (IARC) of the World Health Organisation (WHO), the highest classification consistent with certainty of its carcinogenicity.

Two types of IR health effects are recognised. The severity of *deterministic* effects is directly proportional to the absorbed radiation dose. These effects include skin damage and blood disorders. The higher the dose, the worse, for example, is skin radiation burn. The effects have a threshold below which they do not occur, although this may vary between individuals. This threshold is around 100 mSv at which blood production begins to be impaired. The sievert (symbol: Sv) is the international unit of effective radiation dosage, i.e., 100 mSv is 100 millisieverts.

Stochastic effects are 'probabilistic' in nature. In other words, the higher the dose the greater the chance of them occurring, but once they occur their severity is the same irrespective of the original dose. The main stochastic effect is cancer. The lower the dose of IR, the lower the chance of contracting cancer, but the type and eventual outcome of the cancer is independent of the dose. It can be seen that the high dose deterministic effects of IR were readily observable early after the discovery of radioactivity, but the concept of a stochastic effect as a mechanism for the development of cancer took several decades to be understood. The quantification of stochastic effects has occupied scientific debate throughout most of the 20th century and is still being played out. The distinction is critical to understanding the health impacts of low-dose radiation, particularly with nuclear power and radiation doses to workers and the general population that are below deterministic levels, and to understanding why there is considerable controversy over its significance.

[…]

Nuclear power reactors & cancer

The radioactive burden of nuclear power is not merely from the operation of the power plants. There is an entire nuclear fuel cycle to consider. The potential health impacts of the nuclear fuel cycle not only concern the general public but also nuclear workers.

The nuclear fuel cycle includes the mining and milling of uranium ore; fuel fabrication; production of energy in the nuclear reactor; storage or reprocessing of irradiated fuel; and the storage and disposal of radioactive wastes. The doses to which the public is exposed vary widely from one type of installation to another.

The nuclear reactor core containing nuclear fuel rods, where heat is generated through nuclear fission, is highly radioactive, is heavily shielded, accounting for virtually no ionising radiation from the reactor core to the surrounding region. Every day, however, nuclear reactors routinely produce radioactive gases and liquids that are largely captured and stored on-site until their activity decays to a level sufficient to enable their release into the environment consistent with ensuring the activity is below regulatory limits. Tritium is the largest of the nuclide emissions by activity from civilian reactors, apart from noble gases in some types of reactors. The radioactive effluents almost completely account for all radioactive emissions from nuclear power plants. The per capita dose to regional populations (less than 50 kms) surrounding nuclear power plants is 0.0001 mSv (compared to around 2 mSv natural background dose) and up to 0.02 mSv for specific groups up to 1 km from a nuclear reactor. These are very small doses.

The carcinogenicity of ionising radiation is well established. BEIR VII assigns a risk factor of 5 per cent per Sv, or roughly 1:25000 chance of contracting cancer per mSv dose per annum. On this basis alone, the cancer risk from the documented exposure to ionising radiation from nuclear power stations to the regional general population is 1:250,000,000 per person per annum (or 1:1,250,000 for the specific groups within 1 km of the plant). This would equate to one extra cancer per annum for the whole of the US if the regional population dose was hypothetically generalised to all citizens. Disturbingly however, epidemiological studies are demonstrating much higher cancer rates in selected groups, with the specific causes yet to be determined.

Do nuclear power plants cause cancer in local populations?

The role of civilian nuclear power in the induction of cancer and specifically leukaemia in the general public has been a major controversy over the last three decades and remains unresolved. Leukaemia is malignancy of the blood forming cells and is notable in the context of IR induction in appearing before solid cancers with a latency of around 4 years (compared to >10 years for solid cancers). Although there is little doubt that exposure to radiation increases the risk of developing leukaemia (BEIR VII 2006; Preston et al. 1994; United Nations Scientific Committee on the Effects of Atomic Radiation 2006; IARC 1999), there is disagreement as to whether the amount of exposure received by children living near nuclear sites is sufficient to increase risk.

The first epidemiological study to raise concern of a link was in Great Britain. This addressed an unexpected observed increase in cases of leukaemia in children aged under ten between 1954 and 1983 at Seascale, three kilometres from a reprocessing plant and other nuclear facilities at Sellafield. Published by the epidemiologist, Martin Gardner in 1990, it suggested there was a connection between the increased incidence of leukaemia and Sellafield. Specifically, preconceptional exposures of the fathers of 46 cases of leukaemia, born in west Cumbria and diagnosed there between 1950 and 1985, were compared with those of 564 controls. An association was found between the exposure and leukaemia (Gardner's hypothesis), but this was dominated by four case fathers with high exposure (> 100 mSv). In 1993, a new report by the British Health and Safety Executive found the rate of childhood leukaemia in Seascale was 14 times the national average. Two further studies examined leukaemia clusters in Dounreay and Aldermaston could not correlate paternal exposure levels and leukaemia incidence at these nuclear sites. Furthermore, the increased incidence of leukaemia at Seascale was also occurring in children of unexposed fathers. Additionally, children born outside of Seascale to Sellafield workers did not have an increased incidence to leukaemia. A further study in Canada also failed to demonstrate a link between childhood leukaemia and preconceptional paternal irradiation, or even ambient radiation.

Several studies since 1990 have found mixed results. A congressionally mandated study by the US National Cancer Institute studied the incidence of cancers including leukaemia in 107 counties with nuclear facilities within or adjacent to their boundaries, assessing incidence before and after commencement of operation from 1950-1984. Each county was compared to three similar "control" counties. There were 52 commercial nuclear reactors and 10 Department of Energy facilities. It found no evidence to suggest the incidence of cancer or leukaemia was higher in the study counties compared to the control counties. It did, however, acknowledge shortcomings in its methodology, including not accounting for the potential for 'at risk' populations to be smaller than the specific county study populations, and thus potentially masking underlying increases. Many other studies did confirm increased rates of childhood leukaemia in proximity to nuclear power plants. But they could not confirm a correlation with radiation dose and therefore the link was uncertain.

A 2007 meta-analysis of 17 research studies involving 136 nuclear sites in the UK, France, USA, Spain, Japan, Germany and Canada of the incidence and mortality of childhood cancer in relation to their proximity to nuclear power plants confirmed an increased incidence of leukaemia. The significance of this meta-analysis is that it not only stratified the distance from the nuclear plants, albeit in coarse terms, but also stratified the age groups of children, arguing that since the peak susceptibility to childhood leukaemia is under the age to ten, this group should be independently assessed. Any broader age groups could conceal an increase in incidence. They found in children up to 9 years old, leukaemia death rates were from 5 to 24 per cent higher, and leukaemia incidence rates were 14 to 21 per cent higher.

The most recent of these studies and also the most compelling was sponsored by the German government in response to public pressure to examine the issue of childhood leukaemia and nuclear power reactors. This was commissioned by the Federal Office for Radiation Protection (BfS) in 2003. The KiKK case-control study examined all cancers near all of the 16 nuclear reactor locations in Germany between 1980 and 2003, including 1592 under-fives with cancer and 4735 controls, with 593 under-fives with leukaemia and 1766 controls. The main findings were a 0.61-fold increase in all cancers, and a 1.19-fold increase in leukaemia among young children living within 5 kms of German nuclear reactors. These increases were statistically significant and much larger than the cancer increases observed near nuclear facilities in other countries. The study is notable also for measuring the distance of each case from the nuclear reactor so that a distance-risk relationship could be computed. This was the first study of this kind, previous studies having either grouped all cases or coarsely stratified the distance data. The study found not only that risk is greatest closest to the plants but that small increased risk extends up to 70 kms from the nuclear power plant. Their initial conclusions discounted the role of radiation in the development of leukaemia due to the stated emissions being too low. However, an independent review panel appointed by the BfS criticised them for this conclusion, arguing that the dose and risk models assumed by the Kikk authors did not necessarily reflect the actual exposures and possible radiation risks, and thus warranted further research before being dismissed. In other words, they implied that exposure doses might be higher than are currently being measured.

There is reasonably strong evidence now of a link between the proximity of nuclear power plants and childhood leukaemia. There is no significant evidence for solid cancers either in children or adults. Clearly further research is warranted, particularly to elucidate the leukaemia causation. Policy makers therefore need to factor this increasingly strong scientific evidence into their decision-making. Legislators considering introducing or expanding nuclear power should consider these health implications. Nuclear regulators also need to revisit their assumptions and consider revising standards at existing nuclear plants.

[…]

Conclusion

The nuclear power industry is bedevilled with a military pedigree responsible for the worst weapons of mass destruction. The industry's marketing gurus would say they have a "branding" problem. The nuclear power industry would also distance itself from this pedigree, claiming that it has an impeccable record of operational safety. The evidence contradicts their claims and underscores much of the uncertainty that shrouds their estimates for future safety. The "branding" problem is ironic, since the creation of a nuclear power industry was an attempt to rebrand the nuclear weapons industry and give it legitimacy and cultivate public support by emphasising the perverse dichotomy of the need to prepare for nuclear war and the peaceful promise of the energetic atom—a "peace now, war later" scenario.

The enthusiastic public relations driven motives of politicians and the military to pursue nuclear power presupposed the development and expansion of nuclear power, with safety as an afterthought and little tolerance for safety and public health concerns. The history of nuclear power is riven with conflicts of interest, understatement of risks, vilification of critics and masterful spin, adapting itself to perennially solving the next environmental problem or energy concern lest it be accused of creating it.

So what is different now? We could facetiously although equally credibly argue not much, for the nuclear power industry has now put its hand up to solve the environmental problem du jour, climate change, with claims of cost effectiveness and safety. The rhetoric is redolent of its 1970s mantra of saving us from fossil fuel pollution and establishing energy independence, just before the Three Mile

Island and later Chernobyl accidents. Ultimately, the disastrous economic incompetence of the industry was exposed with an expose in Forbes stating that "[t]he [economic] failure of the US nuclear power program ranks as the largest managerial disaster in business history, a disaster on a monumental scale."

Perhaps the most glaring concern is that the nuclear power industry developed with safety concerns trailing a distant second. The science of radiation safety and health effects of ionising radiation were still evolving as the civilian nuclear boosters and industry vested interests encouraged further expansion, the motto being, "electricity now, safety later."

We now have voluminous evidence of public health risks of low levels of ionising radiation, even within occupational regulatory limits. We also know that there is no "safe" level of radiation exposure below which radiation does not lead to a risk of cancer—there is no safe threshold. Although the measured doses on surrounding populations from nuclear power plants are very low, we also have strong evidence of a link between increased rates of childhood leukaemia and proximity to nuclear plants. We acknowledge that nuclear power reactors operate within a nuclear fuel chain that commences with mining of uranium and ends with decommissioning of nuclear reactors, with occupational risks at every step. The long association with uranium mining and lung cancer is unequivocal, due to radon gas exposure. Recent evidence points to radon gas being twice as hazardous as first thought. There is also increasing evidence of an increased rate of solid cancers in nuclear industry workers throughout the nuclear fuel chain proportional to their radiation dose.

Statistical risk modelling to determine nuclear reactor safety has been found wanting and prone to too many uncertainties, leading to orders of magnitude variations in likely reactor accidents. Add to this the potential catastrophic consequences of a core meltdown with failure of containment, and the industry's entreaties of excellence and safety ring hollow. Maybe we should stop listening to them and instead infer from their actions their true beliefs of the likelihood of a major accident—utilities refuse to operate without the liability of a major accident being transferred to tax-payers. Now who really needs protection?

Lastly, the ultimate in public health and safety concern is the intergenerational legacy of billions of tonnes of toxic nuclear fuel waste that needs to be sequestered from the biosphere for hundreds of thousands of years, using questionable statistical modelling of deep geological repositories which have not yet been prepared. Four decades ago, the then-director of the US government's Oak Ridge National Laboratory, Alvin Weinberg, warned that nuclear waste required society to make a Faustian bargain with the devil. In exchange for current military and energy benefits from atomic power, this generation must sell the safety of future generations.

Nuclear Power Is Not a Viable Energy Source

Greenpeace International

In the following viewpoint, Greenpeace International outlines why nuclear energy is not a suitable response to the climate crisis. In response to climate change, the industry has aggressively promoted nuclear power as a solution. On the other hand, greater energy efficiency and renewable energy are viable answers. Nuclear energy diverts needed investment from these sectors. Since renewable energy such as wind and solar produces no radioactive waste, has a low risk of accidents, and does not present any international security challenges, the authors of this study advocate for focusing on these technologies over nuclear energy. Greenpeace is an independent global organization that acts to change attitudes and behavior, protect and conserve the environment, and promote peace.

As you read, consider the following questions:

1. Why does nuclear power generate so much waste?
2. What evidence does the article provide suggesting that nuclear plant accidents are still probable?
3. How is peaceful nuclear power a threat to global security, according to the authors?

Introduction

The nuclear power industry is attempting to exploit the climate crisis by aggressively promoting nuclear technology as a "low-carbon" means of generating electricity. Nuclear power claims to be safe, cost-effective and able meet the world's energy needs. But nothing could be further from the truth.

In fact, nuclear power undermines the real solutions to climate change by diverting urgently needed investments away from clean, renewable sources of energy and energy efficiency. As this briefing outlines, nuclear power is expensive, dangerous and a threat to global security. And, when it comes to combating climate change, it cannot deliver the necessary reductions in greenhouse gas emissions in time; any emissions reductions from nuclear power will be too little, too late and come at far too high a price.

This briefing outlines why nuclear power is a woefully inadequate response to the climate crisis and how, in contrast, renewable energy and greater energy efficiency can deliver in time to tackle climate change, without any of the dangers posed by nuclear power. It also explores the key environmental, health and security issues affecting every stage of the nuclear process: the unsolved problem of radioactive waste; the risk of catastrophic accidents; and the dangers posed to global security. As a typical example, the briefing highlights fundamental problems with the very latest generation of nuclear plants known as the "European Pressurised Reactor".

In defiance of logic, nuclear power has benefited for over half a century from massive financial support in the form of taxpayers' money. Yet it is barely possible to conceive of a more complex and risky way of heating water to produce steam and generate power. It is now time to give priority to simpler, cheaper and more reliable ways of meeting consumer demands for electricity.

The unresolved legacy of nuclear power: radioactive materials—a continuing threat

When atoms are split, a lot of energy is released. Put simply, this is what nuclear energy is. It sounds innocent enough, but nuclear processes produce dangerous radioactive materials. These materials emit radiation that can be very harmful for people and the environment, not only now but also for hundreds of thousands of years to come. Exposure to radioactivity has been linked to genetic mutations, birth defects, cancer, leukaemia and disorders of the reproductive, immune, cardiovascular and endocrine systems.

Commercial nuclear reactors use uranium as fuel. Even before it is ready to be used as fuel, a series of processing steps causes serious environmental contamination. When a uranium atom is split, it produces not only energy but also highly dangerous radioactive waste.

On average, uranium ore contains only 0.1% uranium. The overwhelming majority of the materials extracted during uranium ore mining is waste containing other hazardous radioactive and toxic substances. Most nuclear reactors require one specific form of uranium, uranium-235 (U-235). This form represents only 0.7% of natural uranium. To increase the concentration of U-235, the uranium extracted from ore goes through an enrichment process, resulting in a small quantity of usable 'enriched' uranium and huge volumes of waste: depleted uranium, a toxic radioactive heavy metal Enriched uranium is then put into fuel rods and transported to nuclear reactors where electricity is generated. Nuclear power plant operation transforms uranium fuel into a rich, highly-toxic and dangerous cocktail of radioactive elements, such as plutonium. Plutonium is the manmade element used in nuclear bombs, lethal in minute quantities and dangerous for about 240,000 years.

In contrast to nuclear power, renewable energy is both clean and safe. Technically-accessible renewable energy sources are capable of producing six times more energy than current global demand.

Depleted Uranium (DU) is a by-product of uranium enrichment. Currently a worldwide stock of more than 1.2 million tonnes is stored without any foreseen future use. Britain and the United States used it to provide armour for tanks and piercing tips for munitions in the Gulf War. Despite contravening health physics guidelines, the British and American governments waited years before starting to screen soldiers following their exposure to DU. In 2004, Gulf War veteran Kenny Duncan won a landmark court case against the British government. After years of repeatedly denying that Duncan's ill-health was the result of exposure to DU, the government was forced to recognise the impacts DU had actually had on his health and award him a war pension. Duncan's three children, born after his exposure to DU, suffered health problems similar to those experienced by many Iraqi children. These included immune system suppression and deformed toes.[1] DU continues to be used in arms despite there being no full understanding of its impact on human health and the environment.[2]

Hazardous for hundreds of thousands of years

Nuclear waste is categorised according to both its level of radioactivity and how long it remains hazardous. The International Atomic Energy Agency (IAEA) estimates that, every year, the nuclear energy industry produces the equivalent of about 1 million barrels (200,000m3) of what it considers 'Low and Intermediate-Level Waste' (LILW) and about 50,000 barrels (10,000m3) of the even more dangerous 'High-Level Waste' (HLW).[3] These numbers do not even include spent nuclear fuel, which is a high-level waste too.

Low and Intermediate-Level Waste includes parts of dismantled nuclear power plants (concrete, metals), but also disposable protective clothing, plastics, paper, metals, lters and resins. Low-level and intermediate waste remains radioactive for periods ranging from minutes to thousands of years and needs to be maintained under controlled conditions for these durations.

Even so, large volumes of radioactive waste are discharged in the air and the sea every day.

Extremely dangerous **High-Level Waste** includes materials containing highly-radioactive elements. High-level waste can be radioactive for hundreds of thousands of years and emits large amounts of hazardous radiation. Even a couple of minutes of exposure to high-level waste can easily result in fatal doses of radiation. It therefore needs to be reliably stored for hundreds of thousands of years. Putting this into perspective, humankind has been on Earth for the last 200,000 years, yet it takes 240,000 years for plutonium to be considered safe.

The safe and secure storage of the dangerous waste needs to be guaranteed throughout this period, which potentially spans many Ice Ages. It's no wonder that a solution for dealing with nuclear waste has still not been found.

No solution to radioactive waste

"Reprocessing" creates even more hazardous waste
Some spent nuclear fuel is reprocessed, which means that plutonium and unused uranium are separated out from other waste, with the intention to reuse it in nuclear power plants. A limited number of countries—France, Russia and the UK—conduct reprocessing on a commercial scale. Consequently, dangerous nuclear waste and separated plutonium are repeatedly transported across oceans and borders and through towns and cities.

However, the term "reprocessing" is misleading. The process actually leads to more hazardous waste flows. Only part of the radioactive material is recovered and further processed as nuclear fuel; the rest results in large volumes of various types of radioactive waste that is often dif cult to store. Nuclear reprocessing plants discharge large volumes of radioactive waste on a daily basis with serious environmental impacts. A study published in 2001 showed an increased incidence of leukaemia among under-25 year olds living within 10 kilometres of La Hague nuclear reprocessing plant, in northwest France.[4] According to a 1997 study in the UK, there was twice as much plutonium in the teeth of young people living close to the Sellafield nuclear reprocessing plant than in the teeth of those living further away.[5]

Reprocessing of nuclear waste endangers our health and does not decrease the radioactive waste problem. It has been estimated that, over the next 40 years, the radioactive discharges of the Rokkasho reprocessing plant, to be started in Japan, will be very large relative to other nuclear operations and will lead to exposure of members of the public to radiation equivalent to half of that released during the Chernobyl catastrophe.[6]

Burying the problem?

The nuclear industry wants to bury the problem of radioactive waste by storing it in deep geological repositories. However, not a single one has yet been built. It appears to be impossible to find suitable locations where safety can be guaranteed for the timescales necessary.

Construction of the Yucca Mountain waste site in Nevada, in the United States, began in 1982, but the date for start of operation has been postponed from 1992 to beyond 2020. The US Geological Survey has found a fault line under the planned site[7] and there are serious doubts about the long-term future movements of underground water that can transport deadly contamination into the environment. Proposals for an underground dump in Finland suffer from similar concerns.

Given the immense difficulties and risks associated with the storage of dangerous nuclear waste, it's not surprising that the nuclear industry tries to dump it out of sight. One such example is Russia—during the Soviet era, nuclear facilities were built in closed cities (in, for example, the Urals and Siberia), resulting in a history of nuclear disasters, environmental contamination and public health scandals, all of which were kept secret by the Soviet government. One of these cities, Mayak, may now be the most radioactively contaminated place on Earth. Despite its appalling record of managing nuclear waste, Russia wants to import foreign nuclear waste for storage and/or reprocessing at Mayak, as well as other sites.

Despite the billions already invested in research and development for dealing with radioactive waste, new experiments are still being presented as "solutions"; methods that will not be ready for a long time, may never be commercially viable or do little to solve the long term waste problem.

Measures to improve energy efficiency are available now. According to Amory Lovins of the US-based Rocky Mountain Institute, "Each dollar invested in electric efficiency displaces nearly seven times as much carbon dioxide as a dollar invested in nuclear power, without any nasty side effects."[8]

Accidents: A complex and uncontainable risk

On 26 April 1986, an accident at the Chernobyl nuclear plant in the Ukraine caused a meltdown in the reactor, resulting in the release of more radioactivity than that spread when the atom bombs were dropped on Hiroshima and Nagasaki. Chernobyl is marked in history as the world's worst civilian nuclear disaster. During the disaster, 56 people died and about 600,000 people were exposed to signi cant levels of radiation. Radioactive contamination spread to places as far away as Lapland and Scotland[9]. Hundreds of thousands of people in contaminated regions had to abandon their homes.

Radioactive pollution has long-term impacts on health. The precise death toll from Chernobyl will never be known but it may exceed 90,000 people.[10] As former UN Secretary General Kofi Annan was reported as saying on the twentieth anniversary of the accident, "seven million people are still suffering, everyday." Three million children require treatment and many will die prematurely.[11]

The nuclear industry argues that the Chernobyl catastrophe was only the result of old technology and mismanagement within the old Soviet bloc. Yet nuclear accidents and "near misses," in which the fuel rods at the core of a reactor come close to melting down, continue to occur in nuclear plants around the world.

Our Insatiable Energy Consumption

We need energy most of the time in our daily life. In pursuit of better living standards, we inadvertently and constantly consume an abundant amount of energy: The demand on primary energy increased from 572,684 terajoules in 2001 to 580,753 terajoules in 2011 in Hong Kong while the total annual electricity consumption also increased from 130,675 terajoules to 151,432 terajoules* (Census and Statistics Department, 2012), and the population also increased from approximately 6.7 million to over 7 million. In addition, the rapid development and widespread usage of information technology also put pressure on energy supply. Energy supply is therefore, one of the most important social issues related to the environment, stability, price, safety, social acceptance and other factors.

Hong Kong and other places in the world are all facing the problem of energy supply. Oil and other resources became important bargaining chip in international politics, and triggered numerous regional disputes. In addition, a 9.0 magnitude earthquake broke out in the eastern coast of Japan on 11th March 2011. The subsequent tsunami damaged the Fukushima Daiichi Nuclear Power Plant and led to a nuclear accident. The accident ignited a new round of energy problems and safety of nuclear power is now being reconsidered by many countries. Renewable energy development is often constrained by regional environmental factors. The above situation revealed that the energy supply problem has reached to a crossroad. We have to find an appropriate solution immediately.

"The Alternatives to Fossil Fuel," Environmental Campaign Committee.

Since Chernobyl, there have been nearly 200 "near misses" in the US alone, according to the US Nuclear Regulatory Commission (NRC).[12] Another example involved a serious technical failure in the Forsmark nuclear power plant in Sweden, in 2006, which forced four of the country's six reactors to shut down. A former director of the plant said, "It was pure luck that there was not a meltdown... it could have been a catastrophe."[13] Also in 2006, one-third of the control rods in a pressurised water reactor at the Kozloduy plant, in Bulgaria, failed to operate during an emergency shutdown.

In 1999, workers failed to follow guidelines at the Tokaimura nuclear fuel plant in Japan, leading to an uncontrolled nuclear chain reaction. Two workers received lethal doses of radiation, and the neighbourhood had to be evacuated. The IAEA concluded that serious breaches of safety principles were the cause of the accident.[14] Operational shortcuts had been taken to make the process quicker and cheaper.[15]

Even if technology never failed and human operators never made errors, natural disasters still present significant risks. In 2003 the French nuclear safety agency activated its emergency response centre following torrential rainfall along the lower Rhone River, which threatened to flood two nuclear reactors at the Cruas-Meysse power plant.[16]

In 2007, an earthquake in Japan caused a fire at the Kashiwazaki-Kariwa nuclear power plant. The earthquake caused its seven reactors to shut down, releasing cobalt-60 and chromium-51 into the atmosphere from an exhaust stack and leading to 1,200 litres of contaminated water leaking into the sea.[17] A year later all seven reactors were still inoperable.

Nuclear power gambles with our lives, health and environment, while a sustainable energy future without these risks is at hand. Greenpeace and the European Renewable Energy Council (EREC) commissioned the DLR Institute (German Aerospace Centre) to develop a global sustainable energy pathway to 2050. The resulting "Energy [R]evolution" blueprint[18] shows that if, intelligent policy and infrastructure choices are made now, renewable energy and energy efficiency could provide half of global energy requirements by 2050 and reduce use of fossil fuels to 30%. The scenario clearly shows that the necessary reduction in CO_2 emissions can be obtained without nuclear power.

A threat to global security

Nuclear power evolved from the atomic bomb, and the two have remained connected ever since. One of the most fundamental and insoluble problems of nuclear power is that the enriched uranium it burns, and the plutonium it produces, can be used to construct nuclear weapons. Other radioactive products formed in nuclear reactors can be used to produce dirty bombs.

A typical nuclear power plant produces sufficient plutonium every year for 10–15 crude nuclear bombs.[19] Former UN Secretary-General Kofi Annan warned, in 2005, that using such nuclear bombs "would not only cause widespread death and destruction, but would stagger the world economy and thrust tens of millions of people into dire poverty."[20]

Experiments by the US government have shown that several nuclear weapons can be built in a matter of weeks using ordinary spent fuel from light water reactors (the most common type of reactors). One study revealed that a country with only a minimal industrial base could quickly and secretly build a small plant, just 40 metres long, capable of extracting about a bomb's worth of plutonium every day.[21]

This relationship between bombs and electricity generation is reinforced by the dual roles of the IAEA in both policing nuclear technology to halt the spread of nuclear weapons and promoting nuclear power. Dominique Voynet, French Senator and former Minister for the Environment, points out: "The IAEA acts as a true promoter for the nuclear industry worldwide. By deliberately ignoring the interlink between civil and military nukes, it contributes to the proliferation of missile materials."[22] We do not need to look far for examples of how this approach has failed to stop the spread of nuclear weapons. China, India, Iraq, Israel, North Korea, Pakistan and South Africa have all used their nuclear power industry to covertly develop nuclear weapons programs.

Forty other countries, currently without nuclear weapons programmes but which have experimented with or developed nuclear power, have access to the nuclear materials and technology needed to make a nuclear bomb.[23]

Vulnerable to terrorists

Despite extensive treaties and political efforts, effectively safeguarding nuclear materials and technology against terrorist threats remains an impossible task. Mohamed El Baradei, head of the IAEA and the man responsible for the safeguards and security regime, admitted in 2005 that, "Export controls have failed, allowing a black market for nuclear material to develop, a market that is also available to terrorist groups."[24]

Nuclear facilities, as well as the radioactive waste transports that regularly cross countries, are also potential targets for terrorists. For example, reactors have not been built to withstand the impact of a large aircraft; nuclear waste transports are even more vulnerable. A study, written by nuclear expert John Large, evaluated scenarios involving terrorist attacks on, or the crash of, a plutonium shipment from France's La Hague reprocessing plant to the Marcoule reactor. The report estimates that 11,000 people would die from the effects of radiation exposure.[25] A similar study by Dr. Edwin Lyman of the Union of Concerned Scientists finds that a potential terrorist attack on the Indian Point nuclear plant in the US could lead to 518,000 long-term deaths from cancer and as many as 44,000 near-term deaths from acute radiation poisoning.[26]

Nuclear power increases the risk of nuclear weapons capabilities spreading to other countries, of terrorists gaining material to make nuclear bombs and of potential terrorist attacks on nuclear facilities or transports. Renewable energy carries none of these safety or proliferation concerns. It does not require complex safeguards, international bodies, or treaties to police its trade and use. Renewable energy technologies and skills can be easily and safely exported around the world.

Nuclear power is expensive

Nuclear power is often described as "the most expensive way to boil water." Despite its proponents now claiming it to be cost-effective, cost estimates for proposed projects have consistently proved inaccurate. A look at current and past experiences of the anticipated and real costs of nuclear projects reveals an industry in which overspends are prevalent and which is propped up by subsidies.[27] The ratings agency, Moody's, has made it abundantly clear that, even with massive government subsidy, nuclear power is not a sound investment.[28]

The cost of building a nuclear reactor is consistently two to three times higher than the nuclear industry estimates. In India, the country with the most recent experience of nuclear reactor construction, completion costs for the last 10 reactors have, on average, been 300% over budget. In Finland, the construction of a new reactor is already €1.5 billion over budget.

Over the years, billions of dollars worth of taxpayers' money has been poured into nuclear energy, compared to trifling sums that have gone towards promoting clean, renewable energy technologies. In the case of the US, where not one new reactor has been ordered in 30 years, the government tries to tempt private investors with tax credits, federal loan guarantees and contributions to risk insurance.

Nuclear reactors present too large a liability for insurance companies to accept. One major accident, costing hundreds of billions of euros (the total Chernobyl cost is estimated at €358 billion) would bankrupt them. Governments, and ultimately their taxpayers, are forced to shoulder this financial liability. The cost of clean-up after a nuclear power plant closes and the safe management of nuclear waste for many generations are also largely carried by the states instead of the companies themselves.

With a fairer legal and political framework, green electricity can keep the lights on with cleaner, safer, cheaper electricity. Germany's renewable energy industry and the wind industry in Texas are two successful examples that have led to market competitiveness without additional subsidies. Global investment in renewable energy has already doubled in the past three years and there is a corresponding downward trend in cost that makes renewable energy a comparatively cheaper long-term investment. Renewable energy is the cheaper option. To produce double the current amount of nuclear energy would require building 500 Gigawatts (GW) of new capacity taking into account retiring nuclear power plants This could cost USD 4,000 billion[29]. Generating the same amount of electricity (5,200 TWh per year) from renewable sources would require construction of 1,750 GW at the investment of USD 2,500 billion assuming their current costs.[30] This means that nuclear power is 50% more expensive than renewable to build, plus additional costs related to fuel and waste disposal would be avoided

A risk for climate change and energy security

Though some people talk of a "nuclear renaissance" it exists only on paper. Pretentious words and high expectations are not matched by orders for new reactors or by interest from the investment community. Only at nuclear power's peak in 1985 and 1986, the equivalent of 30 new reactors (30 GW) of additional capacity was built per year. In the last decade the average construction rate was just four new reactors (4 GW) per year.

The declining nuclear industry is attempting to latch on to the climate crisis and concerns about energy security, by promoting itself as a "low carbon" solution. Today's world is hooked on coal, oil and gas. Burning these fossil fuels releases carbon dioxide, the main cause of global warming and climate change. Furthermore, oil and gas are nite and concentrated in a limited number of locations around the world, often in unstable regions. This concerns policy makers keen to ensure sufficient and secure supplies of energy for the future.

But, for the simplest of reasons, nuclear energy cannot be a part of a solution: Nuclear power can only deliver too little, too late.

Avoiding the worst impacts of the climate change means that global greenhouse gas emissions need to peak by 2015 and be cut by at least half by 2050, compared to their 1990 levels. This calls for fundamental changes in the way we generate and use electricity.

Even in countries with established nuclear programmes, planning, licensing and connecting a new reactor to the electricity grid typically takes more than a decade.

The Energy Scenario produced by the International Energy Agency shows that, even if existing world nuclear power capacity could be quadrupled by 2050, its share of world energy consumption would still be below 10%. This would reduce carbon dioxide emissions by less than 4%.[31]

Implementation of this scenario would require that one new reactor to be built every 10 days from now until 2050. Investment costs for 1,400 new reactors needed would exceed USD 10 trillion at current prices.[32]

Nuclear power cannot meet concerns about energy security either. The 439 commercial nuclear reactors[33] in operation generate around 15% of the world's electricity. This is just 6.5% of the world's total energy supply. Nuclear power only generates electricity. Any contribution to hot water and central heating supply would be marginal, and it does not meet our transport needs at all.[34]

Nuclear power plants depend on uranium for fuel, an ore found in only a handful of countries. 88% of world production in 2005 was supplied from Australia, Canada, Kazakhstan, Niger, Namibia, Russia and Uzbekistan. Pursuing the so-called "nuclear option" therefore means dependence on a limited source of supply, not contributing to a country's energy independence.

Renewable energy technologies and energy efficiency measures are available now and forever. Construction time for installing a large wind turbine has fallen to only two weeks, with an associated planning period of between one and two years. Harnessing domestic natural resources, a decentralised mix renewable energy and energy efficiency could really provide for more CO_2 reduction and energy security without the hazards of nuclear power.

Endnotes

1 BBC, 3 February 2004, Gulf soldier wins pension fight, http://news.bbc.co.uk/1/hi/scotland /3456433.stm

2 More information on Depleted Uranium use and health impacts: http://www.reachingcriticalwill.org/resources/WILPFNorwayDUreport.pdf http://www.ratical.org/radiation/DU/DUuse+hazard.pdf

3 IAEA Factsheet: Managing Radioactive Waste, 1998. http://www.iaea.org/Publications/Factsheets/English/manradwa.html

4 A-V Guizard, O Boutou, D Pottier, X Troussard, D Pheby, G Launoy, R Slama, A Spira, and ARKM. The incidence of childhood leukaemia around the La Hague nuclear waste reprocessing plant (France): a survey for the years 1978-1998, March 2001. Journal of Epidemiol Community Health 2001;55:469-474 (July)

5 O'Donnell, Mitchell PI, Priest ND, Strange L, Fox A, Henshaw DL and Long SC (1997). Variations in the concentration of plutonium, strontium-90 and total alpha-emitters in human teeth collected within the British Isles. Sci Tot Environ, 201, 235–43.

6 Dr Ian Fairlie, Estimated Radionuclide Releases and Collective Doses from the Rokkasho Reprocessing Facility http://www.greenpeace.or.jp/campaign/nuclear/images/n0800206_en.pdf

7 Keith Rogers, Las Vegas Review–Journal, 24 September 2007, Yucca fault line might spring surprise, http://www.lvrj.com/news/9954856.htm

8 Guardian, 12th August 2004, "Nuclear Plants Bloom" by John Vidal, http://www.guardian.co.uk/life/feature/story/0,,1280884,00.html

9 De Cort et al, 1998 (Atlas of Caesium Deposition on Europe after the Chernobyl Acciden EUR Report 16733. Of ce for Of cial Publications of the European Communities, Luxembourg.)

10 Estimations of the death toll vary. The IAEA's estimates 4000 whereas a Greenpeace study found gures of approximately 93,000 fatal cancer cases caused by Chernobyl in Belarus and during the last 15 years, 60,000 additional fatalities in Russia because of the Chernobyl accident. The Chernobyl Catastrophe—Consequences on Human Health, Greenpeace, 2006. http://www.greenpeace.org/international/press/reports/chernobylhealthreport

11 Associated Press, Worst Effects of Chernobyl to come, Geneva, 25 April 2000

12 An American Chernobyl: Nuclear Near Misses at U.S. Reactors Since 1986 13 The Local, Nuclear Plant could have gone into meltdown, 1 August 2006 http://www.thelocal.se/4487/20060801/

14 International Atomic Energy Agency, Report on the preliminary fact nding mission following the accident at the nuclear fuel processing facility In Tokaimura, Japan 1999. http://f40.iaea.org/worldatom/Documents/Tokaimura/iaea-toac.pdf

15 Shigehisa Tsuchiya,PhD, A.Tanabe, T Narushima,K.Ito and K Yamazaki; Chiba Institute of Technol ogy, An Analysis of Tokaimura Nuclear Criticality Accident:A Systems Approach. 2001

16 http://www.ben eldhrc.org/activities/cat_reports/cat_report4/pages/fr_ .htm

17 David McNeill,The Independent: Fear and fury in shadow of Japan's damaged nuclear giant, 21 July 2007.

18 Energy Revolution-A Sustainable World Energy Outloook, Greenpeace and European Renewable Energy Council, January 2007- http://www.greenpeace.org/international/press/reports/energy-revolution-a-sustainab

19 Based on average nuclear power plant production of 10-15 tonnes of Spent Fuel a year. One tonne of spent nuclear fuel typically contains about 10 kilogrammes of plutonium—enough for a crude nuclear bomb

20 Annan: Nuclear Terror a Real Risk, 10 March 2005 http://news.bbc.co.uk/1/hi/world/europe/4336713.stm

21 Since 1977, US nuclear research labs extensively studied the feasibility of developing a 'quick and dirty' reprocessing plant. Most of the original documents remain classi ed, but an excellent overview has been published by V. Gilinsky et al. in 2004 (V. Gilinsky et al., A fresh examination of the prolif eration risks of Light Water Reactors was published by the Nonproliferation Policy Education Centre, October 2004). The rst major study proved

that a country with a minimal industrial base could quickly and secretly build a small reprocessing plant, capable of extracting about a bomb's worth of plutonium per day.
22 http://www.greenpeace.org.uk/tags/ko -annan, 11 April 2006
23 George Jahn, Associated Press,UN: 40 nations have nuclear weapon capabilities in the Oakland Tribune, September 21, 2004 http:// ndarticles.com/p/articles/mi_qn4176/ is_20040921/ai_n14585583 Jeanna Bryner, LiveScience ,Small Nuclear War Would Cause Global Environmental Catastrophe 11 December 2006 http://www.livescience.com/ environment/061211_nuclear_climate.html
24 Spiegel Magazine 8 December 2005: Keeping the World Safe from the Bomb.
25 Large and Associates, 2 March 2004 "Potential Radiological Impact and Consequences Arising From Incidents Involving a Consignment of Plutonium Dioxide Under Transit From Cogema La Hague to Marcoule/Cadarache"
26 Dr Edwin Lyman, Union of Concerned Scientists for Riverkeeper, Chernobyl-on-the-Hudson?: The Health and Economic Impacts of a Terrorist Attack at the Indian Point Nuclear Plant September 2004. http://riverkeeper.org/campaign.php/indian_point/ we_are_doing/980
27 Stephen Thomas, Peter Bradford, Antony Froggatt and David Milborrow, The economics of nuclear power, May 2007 http://www.greenpeace.org/international/press/ reports/the-economics-of-nuclear-power
28 Special Comment Credit Risks and Bene ts of Public Power Utility Participation in Nuclear Power Generation Summary Opinion, Moody's June 2007
29 Based on investment estimates by Moody's of 7,500 USD/kW installed capacity. "New Nuclear Generation in the United States: Potential Credit Implications for U.S. Investor Owned Utilities Moody's Corporate Finance, May 2008.
30 Renewable gures based on parameters given in the Energy Revolution Scenario. www.greenpeace.org/energyrevolution
31 Energy Technology Perspectives 2008, IEA/OECD, June 2008.
32 Figures based on Moody's estimate of nuclear power 7,500 USD/KW.
33 IAEA Power Reactor Information System, October 2008 http://www.iaea.org/ programmes/a2/
34 International Energy Agency, World Energy Outlook 2006. However, other analysis by the International (IIASA) shows that nuclear power represents only 2.2% of world energy consumption. This is because the IIASA considers the electric output of a nuclear plant a primary energy source. The IEA on the other hand considers heat the primary energy source and then assumes 33% ef ciency. Consequently, the value in primary energy of a kWh of nuclear power produced today according to IIASA's methodology is roughly one third of that of the same kWh according to the IEA methodology.

Periodical and Internet Sources Bibliography

The following articles have been selected to supplement the diverse views presented in this resource.

Chatham House, "Nuclear Energy After Fukushima," https://www. chathamhouse.org/research/topics/energy/energy-security/ nuclear-energy-after-fukushima?gclid=CJLNp-abstICFQx_ fgode_UPgg.

European Commission, "Nuclear Energy," https://ec.europa.eu/ energy/en/topics/nuclear-energy.

Dave Levitan, "Is Nuclear Power our Energy Future, Or in a Death Spiral," Climate Central, March 6, 2016, http://www. climatecentral.org/news/nuclear-power-energy-future-or- dinosaur-death-spiral-20103.

John McCarthy, "Frequently Asked Questions About Nuclear Energy," http://www-formal.stanford.edu/jmc/progress/nuclear-faq.html.

New York Times, "Nuclear Energy," https://www.nytimes.com/topic/ subject/nuclear-energy.

Nuclear Energy Institute, "FAQ About Nuclear Energy," https://www. nei.org/Knowledge-Center/FAQ-About-Nuclear-Energy.

Office of Nuclear Energy, https://www.energy.gov/ne/office-nuclear- energy.

Power: Business and Technology for Global Generation, http://www. powermag.com/category/nuclear/.

Union of Concerned Scientists, "How Nuclear Power Works," http:// www.ucsusa.org/nuclear-power/nuclear-power-technology/how- nuclear-power-works#.WLUCuSMrIy4.

For Further Discussion

Chapter 1

1. Should we continue to invest in nuclear power over renewable energy? Why or why not? Does your answer vary between industrialized and developing nations? If so, why?
2. Since the technologies are closely related, peaceful nuclear projects often lead to nuclear weapons, as we have seen in India and Pakistan—and possibly Iran. Do you think the United States and the international community can enable nuclear energy without risking weapons proliferation? Is the trade-off worth it?

Chapter 2

1. Early US efforts to promote nuclear power, such as Atoms for Peace, were inextricably bound to our nuclear weapons program and national defense priorities. How would you characterize this connection? Do you think it has been successful over the long term? Why or why not?
2. What are some of the flaws in the Treaty on the Non-Proliferation of Nuclear Weapons? If you were charged with the responsibility of updating policy, how might you address these flaws?

Chapter 3

1. Some say nuclear plants are vulnerable targets for attack, while others insist nuclear energy is safe. What do you see as the greater threat: nuclear accidents or sabotages, or climate change? In general, how do you view the tradeoff between safety and security and the demand for low carbon energy?
2. What difficulties arise when we try to assess the dangers of nuclear power? Do you trust the various measurements

of radiation proffered by experts? Might there be
hidden dangers?

Chapter 4

1. Nuclear energy may be a way to transcend fossil fuels. It
   provides carbon neutral energy and lacks the supply and
   delivery problems of solar and wind. Others claim that we
   should invest in renewable energy over nuclear power. After
   reading the arguments both for and against nuclear power,
   where do you stand, and why?
2. What rhetorical strategies do opponents of nuclear energy
   use? Are they convincing?

Organizations to Contact

The editors have compiled the following list of organizations concerned with the issues debated in this book. The descriptions are derived from materials provided by the organizations. All have publications or information available for interested readers. This list was compiled on the date of publication of the present volume; the information provided here may change. Be aware that many organizations take several weeks or longer to respond to inquiries, so allow as much time as possible.

Alliance for Nuclear Accountability
202-681-8401
email: jay@nukewatch.org
website: www.ananuclear.org

The Alliance for Nuclear Accountability (ANA) began as an alliance of affected peoples, organizers, health workers, and scientists who wanted to take on a military complex that they believed was poisoning communities, wasting billions of dollars, and putting the world at risk.

American Nuclear Society (ANS)
555 North Kensington Avenue
La Grange Park, Illinois 60526
800-323-3044
website: www.ans.org/contact

The American Nuclear Society is a nonprofit international scientific and educational organization. It was established by a group of individuals who recognized the need to unify the professional activities within the various fields of nuclear science and technology. December 11, 1954, marks the society's historic beginning at the National Academy of Sciences in Washington, DC. ANS has since developed a diverse membership composed of approximately 11,000 engineers, scientists, administrators, and educators representing 1,600 plus corporations, educational institutions, and government agencies.

Beyond Nuclear
6930 Carroll Avenue, Suite 400
Takoma Park, MD 20912
301-270-2209
email: info@beyondnuclear.org
website: www.beyondnuclear.org

Beyond Nuclear aims to educate and activate the public about the connections between nuclear power and nuclear weapons and the need to abandon both to safeguard our future. Beyond Nuclear advocates for an energy future that is sustainable, benign, and democratic. The Beyond Nuclear team works with diverse partners and allies to provide the public, government officials, and the media with the critical information necessary to move humanity toward a world beyond nuclear.

Concerned Citizens For Nuclear Safety
107 Cienega Street
Santa Fe, NM 87501
505-986-1973
email: ccns@nuclearactive.org
website: www.nuclearactive.org

The mission of Concerned Citizens For Nuclear Safety is to protect all living beings and the environment from the effects of radioactive and other hazardous materials now and in the future.

International Atomic Energy Agency
PO Box 100
1400 Vienna, Austria
(+43-1) 2600-0
email: www.iaea.org/contact/official-mail
website: www.iaea.org

The International Atomic Energy Agency is the world's central intergovernmental forum for scientific and technical cooperation in the nuclear field. It works for the safe, secure, and peaceful uses of nuclear science and technology, contributing to international peace and security and the United Nations' Sustainable Development Goals.

Radiation and Public Health (RPHP)
PO Box 1260
Ocean City, NJ 08226
email: odiejoe@aol.com
website: http://radiation.org

The Radiation and Public Health Project is a nonprofit educational and scientific organization established by scientists and physicians dedicated to understanding the relationships between low-level nuclear radiation and public health.

Thorium Energy Alliance
Suite 201
107 W Front St
Harvard, IL 60033
312-303-5019
email: thoriumenergyalliance@gmail.com
website: www.thoriumenergyalliance.com

Thorium Energy Alliance is an educational advocacy organization. A nonprofit group composed of engineers, scientists, and concerned citizens, Thorium Energy Alliance is interested in reducing the cost of energy and protecting the health of the planet and the future of the human race.

United States Nuclear Regulatory Commission (NRC)
US Nuclear Regulatory Commission
Washington, DC 20555-0001
800-368-5642
website: www.nrc.gov

The US Nuclear Regulatory Commission (NRC) was created as an independent agency by Congress in 1974 to ensure the safe use of radioactive materials for beneficial civilian purposes while protecting people and the environment. The NRC regulates commercial nuclear power plants and other uses of nuclear materials, such as in nuclear medicine, through licensing, inspection, and enforcement of its requirements.

Weinberg Foundation
5 Rowan House
Maitland Park Road
London NW3 2EY
United Kingdom
+44 (0)7941 433780
email: www.the-weinberg-foundation.org/contact
website: www.the-weinberg-foundation.org

The Alvin Weinberg Foundation works with NGOs, policy-makers, researchers, and industry to lead the debate on the need for urgent research into next-generation nuclear energy in general and thorium and Molten Salt Reactors in particular.

World Nuclear Organization
Tower House
10 Southampton Street
London WC2E 7HA
United Kingdom
+44 (0)20 7451 1520
email: info@world-nuclear.org
website: www.world-nuclear.org

The World Nuclear Organization is the international organization that represents the global nuclear industry. Its mission is to promote a wider understanding of nuclear energy among key international influencers by producing authoritative information, developing common industry positions, and contributing to the energy debate.

Bibliography of Books

David Bodansky, *Nuclear Energy: Principles, Practices, and Prospects.* New York, NY: Springer, 2008.

Paul Bracken, *The Second Nuclear Age.* New York, NY: Henry Holt, 2012.

Kate Brown, *Plutopia: Nuclear Families, Atomic Cities, and the Great Soviet and American Plutonium Disasters.* New York, NY: Oxford University Press, 2013.

Frank Close, *Nuclear Physics: A Very Short Introduction.* Oxford UK: Oxford University Press, 2015.

Gweneth Cravens and Richards Rhodes, *Power to Save the World: The Truth About Nuclear Energy.* New York, NY: Vintage Books, 2007.

Charles D. Ferguson, *Nuclear Energy: What Everyone Needs to Know.* New York, NY: Oxford University Press, 2011.

Ian Hore-Lacy, *Nuclear Energy in the 21st Century.* London, UK: World Nuclear University Primer, 2012.

Maxwell Irvine, *Nuclear Power: A Very Short Introduction.* Oxford: Oxford University Press, 2011.

Naoto Kan and Jeffrey S. Irish, *My Nuclear Nightmare: Leading Japan through the Fukushima Disaster to a Nuclear-Free Future.* Tokyo, Japan: Gentosha Inc., 2012.

Mark Lynas, *Nuclear 2.0: Why a Green Future Needs Nuclear Power.* Cambridge, UK: Amazon Kindle Single, 2013.

James Mahaffey, *Atomic Accidents: A History of Nuclear Meltdowns and Disasters: From the Ozark Mountains to Fukushima.* New York, NY: Pegasus Books, 2015.

Richard Martin, *SuperFuel: Thorium, the Green Energy Source for the Future.* New York, NY: St. Martin's Press, 2012.

Tony Seba, *Clean Disruption of Energy and Transportation: How Silicon Valley Will Make Oil, Nuclear, Natural Gas, Coal, Electric Utilities and Conventional Cars Obsolete by 2030.* (Self-Published) 2013.

Ken Silverstein, *The Radioactive Boy Scout: The Frightening True Story of a Whiz Kid and His Homemade Nuclear Reactor.* New York, NY: Villard, 2005.

Charles E. Till and Yoon Il Change, *Plentiful Energy: The Story Of The Integral Fast Reactor: The Complex History Of A Simple Reactor Technology, With Emphasis On Its Scientific Bases For Non-Specialists*. Charleston, SC: CreateSpace, 2012.

William Tucker, *Terrestrial Energy: How Nuclear Energy Will Lead the Green Revolution and End America's Energy Odyssey*. Baltimore, MD: Bartleby Press, 2008.

J. Samuel Walker, *Nuclear Energy and the Legacy of Harry S. Truman* (Truman Legacy Series). Kirksville, MO: Truman State University Press, 2016.

Tom Zoellner, *Uranium: War, Energy, and the Rock That Shaped the World*. New York, NY: Penguin, 2010.

Index